Negotiate Like a Phoenician

Discover TraDEAbLes™

by Dr. Habib Chamoun-Nicolás

in collaboration with

Randy Doyle Hazlett, PhD

Chamoun-Nicolás

Copyright © 2008 Keynegotiations
All rights reserved

No part of this publication may be reproduced, stored in a retrieval system or transmitted in any form or by any means electronic, mechanical, photocopying, recording or otherwise, without the prior written permission of Dr. Habib Chamoun-Nicolás.

Library of Congress Control Number: 2007900290

International Standard Book Number

ISBN-13: 978-0-9792073-2-7

Printed in the United States of America

1st Printing

Special Hardcover Edition

TraDEAbLes™

Limit of Liability / Disclaimer of Warranty: While the publisher and the author have used their best efforts in preparing this book, they make no representations or warranties with respect to the accuracy or completeness of the contents of this book and specifically disclaim any implied warranties of merchantability or fitness for a particular purpose. No warranty may be created or extended by sales representatives of written sales materials. The advice and strategies contain herein may not be suitable for your situation. You should consult a professional when appropriate. Neither the publisher nor the author shall be liable for any loss of profit or any other commercial damages, included but not limited to special, incidental, consequential or other damages.

All scripture quotations, unless otherwise indicated, are taken from the HOLY BIBLE, NEW INTERNATIONAL VERSION®. NIV®. Copyright ©1973, 1978, 1984 by International Bible Society. Used by permission of Zondervan. All rights reserved.

On the cover: A Phoenician coin. Dishekel with war galley and hippocamp. Minted in Byblos c. 350-333 BCE.
Original photography courtesy of Salim George Khalaf,
http://phoenicia.org.

Cover art design:
Randy Doyle Hazlett
Inspired by the artwork of Monte Maestru

Dedication

To all those who believe it possible to have win-win outcomes in life. May your actions reflect this belief as you step up to lead this generation.

You must give some time to your fellow men. Even if it's a little thing, do something for others – something for which you get no pay but the privilege of doing it.

Albert Schweitzer

TraDEAbLes™

What the experts are saying

Ever wondered what you might learn about negotiation by studying the Bible? As it turns out, according to Dr. Habib Chamoun, quite a lot. The Hebrew Scriptures actually offer negotiating texts – all derived from the Phoenician business model. And, using a system he calls "Tradeables™," Dr. Chamoun shows how this ancient wisdom applies in a wide range of contemporary business settings. There's even an appendix analyzing the benefits of on-line negotiation instruction and other teaching technologies. If you are looking for historical insights that will help you improve your business negotiations, this is the book for you.

Lawrence Susskind
Ford Professor, Massachusetts Institute of Technology

I continue to be impressed by and learn from Habib Chamoun-Nicolás' insights into negotiation. He has creatively expanded core theoretical principles while also keeping his feet firmly on the ground. His ability to integrate theory and practice has made an important contribution to our field.

Michael Wheeler
Professor, Harvard Business School
Editor of the Negotiation Journal

In his new book, *Negotiate Like a Phoenician*, Dr. Habib Chamoun sounds like he lived with those masters of the seas and professional negotiators, and went with them from harbor to harbor and negotiated the traded goods. This book is not only about negotiation, but it is a part of a new domain in history known as the history of daily life. Thanks for this new reference in History, Negotiation and Business.

Georges Ch. EL-HAJJ
Archaeologist,
Beirut, Lebanon

Chamoun-Nicolás

Office of the Bishop
Eparchy of Our Lady of Lebanon
Maronite Catholic Diocese

October 15, 2007

Habib Chamoun-Nicolás, Ph.D.
Keynegotiations
P.O. Box 6558
Kingwood, Texas 77345

Dear Dr. Chamoun-Nicolás,

    Thank you for the opportunity to review your latest book, *Negotiate Like a Phoenician*.

    Our late Holy Father, Pope John Paul II, was masterful in teaching that respect for the dignity of the human person is a foundational principle of scripture - of God's relationship with His people - and therefore should be the foundation of our relationships with one another. *Negotiate Like a Phoenician* reaches back through historical-scriptural case studies, examining the fabric of ancient commerce to bring this fundamental principle forward, making it a core value for contemporary personal and business relationships. I thank you for making such a resource available and accessible to a wide range of professions. I am sure that all who read this book will profit from its contents.

    May the Lord bless you with much success and a fruitful harvest as you continue to spread this "good news" about the world and the kind of dignified human interaction it could behold once again.

    With prayerful best wishes, I am

Sincerely yours in Christ,

Most Reverend Robert J. Shaheen
Bishop of the Diocese of Our Lady of Lebanon

TraDEAbLes™

Those of us that have closely followed Habib Chamoun-Nicolás' career recognize and value his talent evident in his work like: *Deal, Trato Hecho, Desarrollo de Negocios* and his many conferences, seminars, and assessment programs presented around the world.

In *Negotiate Like a Phoenician,* his latest work, he portrays an extremely well-planned and profound dimension on a civilization and the events that evolve in it. Throughout this work, he presents clues of human nature, not only of man in our time, but also of past and future times.

From the beginning of the book, in the dedication, he expresses feelings of general wellbeing, where exclusion and prejudice have no place among human relationships. The best alternative is to win-win, not only as a way to generate excellent and meaningful relationships, but also as a way of life.

Sometimes the speed at which events develop makes us lose sight of this viewpoint, and we cannot appreciate success that leaves behind a legacy – a legacy that many times we can neither identify nor benefit from. That is the importance of *Negotiate Like a Phoenician.*

With outstanding argumentation, it values and includes the historic dimension of mankind developed in a clear and succinct way. The clues extracted from successful, real-world negotiations generate the interesting and productive notion of Tradeables™. This text, written by one of our most outstanding honorary professors, is an invaluable contribution to the world of business, management, and society in general.

Dr. Michel Doumet Antón
Rector Catholic University of Guayaquil – Ecuador

The Phoenicians conquered the entire Mediterranean Basin without coercion or violence. They did it by intelligence and the power of persuasion. They learned by listening. They discovered where the trade winds and best harbors were located, how to build better boats, how to navigate by the stars and moon, how to share important information (they created the first alphabet), they learned the likes and dislikes of the peoples around them, and lastly they knew how to bring themselves *and others* benefit.

Habib Chamoun-Nicolás shows us how to learn the same art from the ancient Phoenicians. Intelligence, persuasion, and care for the good of others worked then and still works today.

Bishop Gregory John Mansour
Bishop of St Maron of Brooklyn
For the Maronites

Dr. Habib Chamoun-Nicolás' new book, Tradeables™, provides an intriguing account of ancient negotiation techniques developed by the Phoenicians in 2000 BCE and shows how such techniques can be used in a practical manner by today's negotiators. Dr. Chamoun-Nicolás, explains the importance of an international negotiator being "flexible, open, stereotype-free, and, most of all, patient and tolerant," and why the Phoenicians' great success as international traders was based on their belief that "honesty was the best policy" when negotiating with others. In my opinion, Tradeables™ ought to be considered a "must read" for every teacher or practitioner involved in the art of negotiation.

Judge Frank G. Evans
Recognized Father of Alternative Dispute Resolution (ADR) in Texas
Founder of the Frank G. Evans Center for Conflict Resolution at
South Texas College of Law

Dr. Chamoun-Nicolás' book *Negotiate Like a Phoenician* introduces us to Tradeables™ as a Phoenician (Canaanite) business practice, showing that successful business practice based upon scientific principles has flourished over the centuries by nations around the world up to our times. The Phoenicians (Canaanites) were pioneers in that field over the ages. Dr. Chamoun was very successful in sorting out these principles from various sources and synthesizing them into a practical theory. These principles (cultural sensitivity, ingenuity, adventurous spirit, fair play, clarity in communications, etc.) are still behind business excellence of nations today. This book proves to be an excellent coronation for that practiced theory and an outstanding reference for businessmen and historians alike. Dr. Chamoun-Nicolás has to be congratulated for producing another outstanding work.

Hazem Chahine
Senior Lecturer, Faculty of Engineering,
American University of Beirut
Former Inspector General, Electricity of Lebanon

This is a very insightful book about how to successfully conduct business over the long-term. Dr. Habib provides recounts of business practices of Phoenicians that allowed them to survive and flourish for centuries while neighboring civilizations perished. This book provides great historical information on the negotiations techniques of Phoenicians that can be used in modern day situations.

Adel Chaouch, Ph.D., P.E.
Director, Corporate Social Responsibility
Marathon Oil Company

TraDEAbLes™

Dr. Chamoun is again amazing us with this new teaching tool created to better understand and serve our most demanding customers. His hands-on and writing experiences are evidently distilled into Tradeables™. Every sales, marketing and business development professional will find this book a 'must read'.

To immerse the reader into the real business world, Dr. Chamoun uses metaphors, such as the way the Phoenicians used to negotiate, and step-by-step transports the individual to the customer service environment. *Negotiate Like a Phoenician* teaches effective negotiation skills and covers different dealing situations, like buyer-seller alliances, long-term relationships, and a both-win perspective. A valuable and real toolbox of negotiating expertise.

Leandro Barretto, Ph D
Competency Development Coordinator
Halliburton

I knew Dr. Habib Chamoun in the Paris conference "*New Trends in Teaching Negotiation*" where he was presenting E-learning technology for teaching negotiation. What a nice surprise to see that Dr. Habib, besides using top-level teaching technology, is able to rescue Phoenician trade art, doing a beautiful historical analysis and building a bridge between the very similar old and new negotiation principles. Dr. Habib's book will be very helpful for anyone interested in making a deep dive in negotiation principles. And the diver, for sure, will get fresh and excellent fish.

Gabriel G. da Fonseca
Globaltrande Director

A unique and fantastic book. An excellent resource for all CEOs trying to orchestrate change throughout their organizations and improve corporate and even personal negotiations. I intend to share the book with my clients, associates, and staff, so that together we can gain better insight into different styles and have a better appreciation of the magnitude of effort required to lead the transformation process of negotiations.

Genival Francisco da Silva
President and CEO of Banco Ficsa S A
São Paulo – Brasil

The author blends a rich array of daily life stories with ancient historical examples to aid the reader in taking truly novel concepts from the pages of a book to desired results in business and life – producing win-win outcomes.

Keith Miceli
**Vice President, International Business
Greater Houston Partnership**

When I first received a copy of Dr. Chamoun's new book, I was impressed by the subject that he chose and was curious how the ancient Phoenicians could relate to modern negotiating. Having read *DEAL* recently, I was also willing to discover some new revelation in the art and science of negotiation.

Negotiate Like a Phoenician is an excellent book for laying out the essential skills of successful negotiations, both for new and experienced negotiators, and Tradeables™ happened to be just the revelation I was hoping to find to improve my company and my personal skills.

The well-documented history, illustrated with modern case studies, makes a comprehensive and enjoyable balance that anyone involved in business should put on their list of reference reading.

Carlos Zepeda Chehaibar
**Founding partner & e-business director
Huevocartoon.com Animation Studios**

Readers can always rely on Dr. Chamoun-Nicolás for concise, easy to apply concepts that facilitate real-life negotiations. His new book is no exception. It focuses on tools that will aid any reader in handling business or personal matters with ease and confidence. What he has added now, however, is an interesting, historic 'day trip' to the Mediterranean. There he explores the culture and practices of an ancient civilization to draw conclusions regarding successful negotiation style and methods that are equally applicable today. The journey is both interesting and useful.

Al Amado
Lawyer and International Policy Consultant, Latin American Project, International Institute Director, Frank Evans Center for Conflict Resolution, South Texas College of Law, Houston, Texas, USA

TraDEAbLes™

Habib Chamoun's latest book is a refreshing look at the past ... with an eye to the future. He goes back to the signature Mediterranean traders, the Phoenicians. With that, he comes up with the idea of 'tradeables," (*sic*) which he renders as "traDEAbLes" to remind you of his previous and very successful book, *DEAL*. He ruminates about how the Phoenicians traded and the methods that made them so successful. Chamoun reflects from many of the lessons learned from the Phoenicians and gives us a marvelous opportunity to hone our negotiating skills. Congratulations again to Dr. Habib Chamoun-Nicolás for his latest, *TraDEAbLes*.

Rodolfo J. Cortina, Ph.D.
Professor & Director University of Houston Center for the Americas
Coordinator, University of Houston-MA/MBA Program
Former UHS Vice Chancellor for International Affairs
Former President American College of Acupuncture & Oriental Services

The art of negotiation is as ancient as human history. In this book, Dr. Habib Chamoun reveals the thread which binds the negotiation examples from the Bible with contemporary societies, and you will be astonished by how the ancient negotiation techniques can prove to be perfectly topical, salient, and relevant in today's world. An accurate and well-written book that treats history and negotiation theory with a really interesting and original approach.

Giuseppe De Palo
Chairman of Board, ADR Center (Rome, Italy)
International Professor of ADR Law & Practice, Hamline University School of Law (St. Paul - MN, U.S.A.)

Dr. Habib Chamoun-Nicolás has done a great service to those who wish to learn how best to negotiate in any given situation. His selection of the Phoenicians as models for analysis is a master stroke, and his examples from the Old Testament – my area of expertise – reveal many fresh and startling insights into passages otherwise worn by familiarity. I heartily recommend his book for any seeking to master the necessary skills of negotiation.

Dr. Paul Hahn
Theology Department
University of St Thomas
Houston, Texas 77006

The Hebrew Bible is a rich resource for ideas for modern as well as ancient living. It contains valuable lessons for all time that teach us how to reach for the highest in ourselves.

In *Negotiate Like a Phoenician*, Dr. Habib Chamoun-Nicolás discovers yet another dimension in the text – lessons not just for honesty and fairness in business, but for how to develop and maintain good business relations based, not on theory, but on real-life practicality.

Particularly in his section "Case Studies from the Hebrew Scripture," he demonstrates from descriptions of how business was done between the Phoenicians and Kings David and Solomon how not just honesty, but also honor and mutual respect, are the foundation of business relations that endure. In short, they are good business for all concerned.

Fascinating reading. Interesting ideas. Valuable lessons. Dr. Habib reminds us that while technology and products change, the right and honorable way to do business is eternal and universal.

Rabbi Roy A. Walter
Senior Rabbi, Congregation Emanu El
Houston, Texas

Once again, Habib Chamoun has written a wonderful book. We call it wonderful, as it combines the essentials of negotiation skills together with poignant narratives to illustrate this amazing area of research. Henceforth, it becomes a must have for researchers and practitioners, as well as "negotiation fans".

Drs. Markus Voeth and Uta Herbst
Department of Marketing, University of Hohenheim, Germany

The big lessons of negotiation abilities of Lebanese people are fully valid in the present and give us orientation and projections to the future. Habib Chamoun, with his book, gives us the best tool to learn through time the hard negotiation processes. Thank you for this work that makes us live in a linear way the history of human professional development.

Joseph Garzozi
Director of tourism, international relations and competitiveness
Municipality of Guayaquil

TraDEAbLes™

Negotiating like a Phoenician - a strategy for life. Do you know the importance of drivers, entrapments, analysis and leverage? This evidence-based book is backed by research and draws on biblical accounts. There is sufficient clarity for the MBA student, international diplomats, business negotiators, and those who want to hone their skills for self-development. The work is principle-centred, directing one to the 6Ps of flawless negotiation. There are cross-cultural case studies which entice the reader to explore issues from a win/ win perspective inclusive of clarity of what the negotiator wants, the expectations of the other party, identifying the Tradeables™ and working towards the deal. There is sufficient interest for those negotiating: retail sales, real estate, professional services, advertising, fundraising and negotiating at airports. Develop competence with the principles and see the difference!

Dr. Neslyn Watson-Druée, MBE, FRCN, DUniv, FCGI
Managing Director, Beacon Organisational Development Ltd and Chairman of Kingston Primary Care Trust (UK)

In his book *Deal*, Dr. Habib Chamoun-Nicolás wrote of the elements of cross-cultural negotiations. Here in *Tradeables™*, Dr. Chamoun-Nicolás relates the culture of the Phoenicians and their use of Tradeables™ to create greater negotiation capacity. He makes the case, with historical references, for adhering to Phoenician ways. He contrasts e-learning to face-to-face negotiations. Both interesting and informative, the author's pronouncement of the Phoenician business model is timely and increasingly valuable in today's global markets. Known to outsource when it made sense, the Phoenicians followed seven principles which included a healthy respect for women. It was the Phoenician businessmen, our first "road warriors", who created one of the first international conglomerates. Be prepared to add the concept of Tradeables™ to your next negotiation.

Shelton E. McBride, RPh, COO
Project Rx, Inc.
Houston, Texas, USA

If I had understood Dr. Chamoun's negotiation strategies and use of Tradeables™ 25 years ago when I was negotiating international oil contracts, I would have made much better decisions and "Deals" for my company.

Larry Golden
Retired! Former President of Several Oil and Gas Companies

Hooray for Dr. Habib Chamoun-Nicolás! At last here is a book on negotiating with fresh ideas and stories. As a school boy, I had read about ancient Phoenicia but not about Phoenicians themselves, known as the *Traders of the Sea*. Habib smartly presents his approach to modern negotiating against this Phoenician backdrop. What Sun Tzu's *The Art of War* is to modern strategic business thinking, *Negotiate Like a Phoenician* is to modern negotiating. I hope he writes another book on his CLOSED OPEN principles (Appendix B). I highly recommend Dr. Chamoun-Nicolás's readable book.

Howard Eaton
CEO, Relationship360 Group, LLC

Negotiate Like a Phoenician – Discover Tradeables™ is an immensely enjoyable journey, showing us a fascinating culture of ancient yesterday, ultimately returning us to today with a view of tomorrow's potential. Dr. Habib Chamoun-Nicolás bestows a souvenir of understanding derived from the wisdom of the ages that has broad application to our personal, business and community lives.

The Old Ways may prove to be the Best Ways. This book proves that behaving with integrity is at the core of any Right Way.

Jeff Jury
Burns Anderson Jury & Brenner, L.L.P.
Austin, Texas

This absorbing and interesting book deeply discusses and presents the art of negotiations by introducing a profile of the best known negotiators and traders of human history, the Phoenicians. The knowledge in the field of negotiation and history is presented by the author in a fascinating and direct way. Dr Habib Chamoun-Nicolás recalls the 7 Principles that helped the masters of negotiation approach their high level of trading and which are still current for negotiators these days. He describes in a straightforward and clear way how to find and employ people able to trade efficiently. Apart from reminding us of the ancient Phoenicians, the author shows us how to make use of their wisdom in our businesses. I recommend reading this book to everyone who wants to achieve success in trading.

Wojciech Krakowinski , PhD
The Chairman of the Board of Infinity Group Ltd. (Poland)

TraDEAbLes™

This is a book that intellectually seduces the reader by blending historically successful trading practices from the times of the Phoenicians with those new negotiation tools required by the challenges of current hyper-competitive, highly global knowledge economy.

Dr. Jaime Alonso GOMEZ
National Dean, Professor of Strategy & International Management
Graduate School of Business Administration and Leadership
Tecnologico de Monterrey University System

My first insight appeared on page 2 "...we must recognize what is negotiable, what is not, and what doesn't need to be negotiated" – I knew I was in for a fabulous read! This is no run of the mill how to book - not only is it a guide on managing an effective business life, all the techniques are equally applicable to raising children and managing all the important relationships in our lives. I was drawn into the depth with which Habib built and wove tales and examples like a rich tapestry that so eloquently reveals the lessons. This will be a book worth sharing with all my colleagues who are building their businesses.

Catherine Mossop FCMC
Sage Mentors Inc. (Sagementors.com), Canada

I consider myself a true believer of the sales and negotiation methodologies developed by Dr. Chamoun-Nicolás. After some training, now I am able to achieve better results with some simple steps – Learning how to plan ahead, how to prepare mind-set-maps to develop winner strategies, how to DEAL with difficult people, how to not accept a NO for an answer, how to close in one or two visits. This is something that it is applied successfully everyday at CAIC. When Habib honored me with the opportunity to preview *Negotiate Like a Phoenician*, I was not sure how "old-fashioned" strategies were to be applied in this modern era. Even worse, I was not sure how something that is not within a particular negotiation process can be part of the final outcome. Habib surprised me again with this amazing book. His very particular way to present this new concept "Tradeables™" is the only way a true believer will do it: Teach what you think and believe what you teach. There are Tradeables™ in almost every negotiation…the better you use them, the better you'll do. Think outside the process itself, identify the Tradeables™, and get the DEAL.

Marco A. Contreras
Marketing, Commercial Alliance Insurance Company

Negotiate Like a Phoenician offers very specific techniques and guiding points on how to negotiate and make deals. It uses many examples which facilitate relating described successful real life experiences with your own! The identity given to the word " Tradeables™" is innovative. The amazing thing is that all of this is done using a Biblical context and the way of life of the Phoenicians, a civilization that existed over 2000 years ago!!

Joussef Jerade
COO, Commercial Alliance Insurance Company

The book, *Negotiate Like a Phoenician*, from Dr. Habib Chamoun denotes the wonderful history of human life. It has helped me a lot in my management of business and also matches with our Eastern philosophies. It gave me a good reference in history, negotiation and business.

Minmay Liang
Vice President, Administration & Finance
American College of Acupuncture & Oriental Medicine

As an entrepreneur, I found Dr. Chamoun-Nicolás' latest book, *Negotiate Like a Phoenician*, fascinating. He examines the art of negotiation through the Phoenicians, an ancient society that survived as a culture for centuries, while surrounding nations perished. I especially enjoyed the ancient case studies. The author cleverly shows the reader how to use ancient techniques and apply them today. Dr. Chamoun-Nicolás truly challenges his readers to negotiate like a Phoenician.

Philippe Cras
Owner of Homewood Suites at Kingwood Parc
Kingwood, Texas

This book is a must-read for those who struggle to be winners in their day-to-day negotiations. The 'Chamoun' methodology really works!

Margaret Krakowinska
Student of Aviation Management
London Metropolitan University

Great leaders know the importance of a win-win negotiation and so do the Phoenicians and Habib Chamoun in his new book Tradeables™. Habib Chamoun went back in history to find the essence of negotiation. Building on his foundation book, *DEAL*, he supported his thesis with proof from one of the most respected ancient civilizations: the Phoenicians, the masters of commerce and negotiation. Once again Habib astonishes me with his innovative ideas. Tradeables™ is an excellent guide on how to be an effective, respected and inspiring negotiator.

Ursula EL Hage
Director of the Entrepreneurship School, UCSG

TraDEAbLes™

Special Thanks

I am grateful to GOD for giving me the opportunity and wisdom to share with you my thoughts, feelings, observations, and findings through lifelong experiences, as well as insatiable conversations with multiple experts from diverse backgrounds and nations that unfortunately could not be listed in this manuscript, because it would take another book to write about them. I am very thankful to all of you. God bless you all.

To my better half, my wife and business partner, Marcela, and my four kids, Habib, Emile, Antoine and Marcelle, thanks for your constant support and patience, especially since my career choice requires many sacrifices, and the sacrifice is greater for you than it is for me.

To my long time friend and colleague, Dr. Randy D. Hazlett, without your great contribution, collaboration, and biblical research, this book couldn't turn out to be what it turned out to be – a great book. Thanks to your wife Rose for her continuous support.

Sanford Holst, Dr. Mark McMenamin, Professor Paolo Matthiae, Salim George Khalaf, Joseph Sermarini, Salvatore Dedola, and Peter Solodov, thanks for your contributions and for allowing me to cite your work on Phoenician history and latest findings. Thanks to the Oriental Institute of the University of Chicago for permission to reuse your phenomenal images of ancient bas-relief.

As you may notice, endorsements for this book are coming from great minds all around the globe. I thank all of you for the effort to read the manuscript and honestly write your thoughts for inclusion in this book. Thanks to all:
Al Amado, Dr. Michel Doumet Antón, Dr. Leandro Barretto, Hazem Chahine, Dr. Adel Chaouch, Carlos Zepeda Chehaibar, Georges Ch-EL HAJJ, Marco Contreras, Dr. Rodolfo Cortina, Philippe Cras, Gabriel G. da Fonseca, Genival Francisco da SILVA, Giuseppe De Palo, Howard Eaton, Ursula EL Hage,

Judge Frank Evans, Joseph Garzozi, Larry Golden, Dr. Jaime Alonso Gomez, Dr. Paul Hahn, Dr. Uta Herbst, Joussef Jerade, Jeff Jury, Dr. Wojcieck Krakowinski, Margaret Krakowinska, Minmay Liang, Shelton E. McBride, Keith Miceli, Catherine Mossop, John Raymond Poff, Dr. Larry Susskind, Dr. Markus Voeth, Rabbi Roy A. Walter, Dr. Neslyn Watson-Druée, and Dr. Michael Wheeler,

Some extraordinary people gave me comments to enhance the manuscript or to check for veracity. I am in great debt to you: Norman and Ann Alton, Msgr. Chester L. Borski, Jeff Crandall, Carol Golden, Father Maynard U. Paragan, Emilio Nicolás Saide, Alberto Tohmé, and Father Milad Yaghi.

Thanks to Antoine Gresati Hakim, Lebanese General Counsel of Guadalajara, and the Mexican Lebanese Center of Guadalajara for assistance with the map of ancient Mediterranean colonies.

To my parents, Maria Elena and Habib, thanks for teaching me a love for knowledge and continued education. To my brothers and sister for their support and love, thanks Soraya and Yamal, and to Anuar, who is always in my heart and thoughts.

Specifically on negotiation and technology, special thanks to:

Patricia Aldape Valdes of Monterrey TEC for her technical assistance,
Eng. Carolina Lujambio of Leadership Technologies for her technical assistance on several virtual negotiation coaching sessions,
Eng. Ramon Malpica of CUDEC for his help coordinating a negotiation video conference between Canada and Mexico,
Al Amado, Director for Latin America Frank Evans Center of Conflict Resolution at South Texas School of Law, for providing feedback material, and
Dr. Randy Hazlett, President of Potential Research Solutions, Dallas, Texas, for aid in the preparation of workshop material.

To all my clients, colleagues, workshop participants, and especially to those about to read this book, Thanks.

Habib Chamoun-Nicolás

FOREWORD

I always wonder why every year there are so many new books being published on the subject of negotiation and why should I publish another one. As a paradox, even though there is annual growth in literature on the subject, people are finding it more and more difficult to negotiate. It amazes me the frequency people use force to achieve their negotiation objective rather than using a negotiation procedure. It seems as if human patience is running out. Let's take a look back in human history to examine how people negotiated several thousand years ago, paying special attention to the Phoenicians, known as the *Traders of the Sea* for their mode of business and their successful negotiation skills. Why were they such great negotiators? What were their negotiating techniques? What principles did they follow, and how can we apply those principles today?

While analyzing multiple successful modern negotiations, I discovered a new concept in practice, which I have coined Tradeables™. I also believe using Tradeables™ was an active practice of the ancient culture of the Phoenicians. You will see how such dealings in 2000 BCE are applicable today. We will analyze the seven principles of the Phoenician society, according to historian Sanford Holst in his book, *Phoenicians: Lebanon's Epic Heritage*, and show how to use those same principles to help you find Tradeables™ that can leverage your negotiations.

PROLOGUE

The Phoenicians were Canaanites, the very same Canaanites encountered in Hebrew and Christian scriptures, who reached the height of their cultural influence in about 1000 BCE. The Phoenicians were traders who dominated the sea routes of the Mediterranean, bringing a variety of goods to many markets. Perhaps their greatest achievement was spreading the phonetic alphabet across the ancient world. This greatly simplified the process of business recordkeeping, which Chamoun argues was an important aspect of their success as traders and businessmen.

Those of us living in modern, advanced economies often are in some confusion as to what exactly we want, perhaps because of the sheer abundance of options offered in the marketplace. In contrast, when we look back 3000 years to the Phoenicians, we have the sense that they knew what they wanted and how to get it. They were persistent in achieving their goals.

The Phoenicians focused not so much on price, but more on intangible benefits, which are more valuable than generally believed. They strove to create actual friendships with their business partners, the friendship between Solomon and Hiram being one good example. Chamoun documents this relationship, using many historical sources.

The lesson for the present day businessman is that one should try to think of creative ways to solve the

TraDEAbLes™

client's needs – needs which perhaps are external to the present negotiation. Chamoun coins the term Tradeables™ to capture the essence of this practiced Phoenician concept. The way to discover your customer's unstated needs is to simply ask, then listen. This process itself requires investment, which may be counterintuitive for all of us used to instant results. Chamoun's multi-cultural background makes him a good ambassador for a more holistic approach to negotiating a deal so that both parties leave the table feeling that a fair deal was reached. If contemporary business relationships are akin to ordering ready-made Fillet-O-Fish sandwiches from the McDonald's drive-thru together, the Chamoun way is to go out fishing with your business partner and share the catch over a friendly campfire, perhaps with ample libation and plenty of conversation.

If both parties are not happy, then the negotiation can scarcely be called a success. If only one party is happy, then more likely the "deal" for one party was a "rip off" for the other. This was certainly not the Phoenician way. The idea is not merely to sell a product or service, but to create partnerships. The Phoenicians wanted return business, and therefore pursued long-term relationships. They made sure that their deals benefited their trading partners, as well as themselves. In this way, both parties were anxious to keep the deal, and the relationship, intact.

Negotiating is, or should be, a problem-solving process to provide mutual gains for all. In fact, the Phoenicians frequently would give more than they received in the short term, for the sake of gaining in the long term. Using Tradeables™, the ancient Phoenicians sought to build trust and bring business relationships to a higher level. Read this book, and discover a better way of doing business!

JOHN POFF
U.S. Copyright Office
Library of Congress, Washington, D.C.

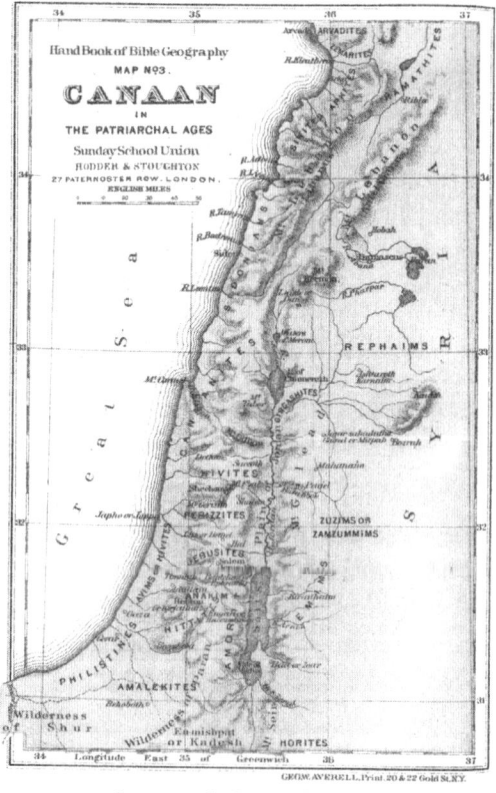

Canaan in the Patriarchal Ages, G. W. Averell
Hand Book of Bible Geography, Map No.3
Hodder & Stroughton, London, 1870

TraDEAbLes™

Reader's Guide

While *Negotiate Like a Phoenician* was carefully organized for a cover-to-cover reading/learning experience, it is recognized that this is no ordinary text. Just fan through the comments of recognized experts if you need to be convinced. This book has drawn accolades from academicians, corporate leaders, and laypeople alike. The commentary and praise cuts across religion and culture. You would be challenged to find another book which extracts time-proven business principles from the annals of a history unknown to most and carries us forward to practical application in today's world. This is neither a history book, a religious exposition, a philosophical dissertation, nor a business textbook, yet *Negotiate Like a Phoenician* contains elements of each. After reading Dr. Chamoun-Nicolás' book, you may be persuaded that business relationships should mirror a world view of global interconnectedness. Today's life is tomorrow's history. *Negotiate Like a Phoenician* challenges you to leave a legacy that future generations will model, whether building a business or a family.

This Reader's Guide on the following page was assembled to customize your study. Just find where you belong and enjoy!

Randy Doyle Hazlett, PhD

Negotiation Expert	Appendix A *Review of 6Ps*	Chapter I *Tradeables™*	Chapter II *7 Principles p. 32*	Chapter III *Moments of Tension, p. 93*	Chapter IV *Tradeables™: How to Produce Them*	Appendix B *Negotiation & Technology*
Negotiation Student	Appendix A *Review of 6Ps*	Chapter I *Tradeables™*	Chapter II *The Ancient Art of Negotiation*	Chapter III *Modern Negotiations*	Chapter IV *Tradeables™: How to Produce Them*	Appendix B *Open/Closed + Technology*
Historian	Chapter I *Tradeables™*	Chapter II *The Ancient Art of Negotiation*	Chapter IV *Tradeables™: How to Produce Them*	Chapter V *Tradeables™: A Phoenician Gift to You*	Appendix B *Negotiation & Technology*	
Entrepreneur	Chapter I *Tradeables™*	Chapter III *Modern Negotiations*	Chapter IV *Tradeables™: How to Produce Them*	Appendix A *Review of 6Ps*	Appendix B *Open/Closed*	
Layperson	Chapter I *Tradeables™*	Chapter II *The Ancient Art of Negotiation (skim quotes)*	Chapter III *Modern Negotiations*	Chapter IV *Tradeables™: How to Produce Them*	Chapter V *Tradeables™: A Phoenician Gift to You*	Appendix B *Open/Closed*

TraDEAbLes™

Table of Contents

Chapter I.   The Hidden Secret to Great Deals:
   TraDEAbLes™ 1
Chapter II. The Ancient Art of Negotiation 9
   Ancient Negotiating Masters 10
   Who Were the Phoenicians? 11
   The Phoenician Business Model 15
   Leveraging Business via Technology 19
      Communication 19
      Construction 19
      Shipbuilding 20
      Navigation 21
      Manufacturing 23
      Mining 23
      Exploration 25
      War 31
   Phoenician Cultural Survival 30
   The 7 Principles of the Best Negotiators Ever 33
   Case Studies from Ancient Historians 37
      Get it in Writing 37
      A Policy of Tribute 39
      A Good Reputation 40
      First Contact Sales or Silent Negotiation 41
      Standing on Principles 42
   Case Studies from Hebrew Scripture 46
      Heritage of the Phoenicians 46
      Tyre – The Marketplace of Nations 46
      Ancient Negotiating Scripts 58
         King David and King Hiram 58
         King Solomon and King Hiram 67
      Commentary Outside the Scriptures 80

Rebuilding the Temple 83
A Counter Example 84
Case Studies from Christian Scripture 86
    The Faith of a Syrophoenician Woman............. 86
    Ending a Quarrel 89
    Summary of Phoenician Negotiating Principles 91
Chapter III. Modern Negotiations and Use of
    Tradeables™ 94
Moments of Tension 95
Anecdote with Multiple Moments of Tension 100
Tradeables™ Case Studies 104
    1) Retail Store Negotiation 105
    2) Real Estate Negotiation 106
    3) Professional Services Negotiation 108
    4) Negotiations in Advertising 109
    5) Fundraising Negotiation 111
Summary 114
Chapter IV. Tradeables™: How to Produce Them ... 115
Chapter V. Tradeables™: A Phoenician Gift to You 164
The Next Generation 167
Negotiate Like a Phoenician 168
Sources 172
Appendix A: Review of analysis methodology from
    *DEAL – Guidelines to a Flawless
    Negotiation*... 174
Negotiation – A Strategy for Life 174
The 6 P's 176
The 6 P's in Action 179
    CASE STUDY A: Trust 179
    CASE STUDY B: Determination 183
    6 P's Analysis Checklist 189
Appendix B: Short Stories and Articles 195

1. Negotiating when you are CLOSED and the other is OPEN 195
2. Negotiation and Technology 205

Suggested Reading 225
About the Collaborator 229
About the Author 230
Contacting the Author 232

Anything we haven't seen before is marvelous.

**Tacitus, *De vita et Moribus*
*Iulii Agricolae***

TraDEAbLes™

Chapter I. The Hidden Secret to Great Deals: TraDEAbLes™

Phoenicians bearing gifts, Persepolis relief, 5th century BCE
Courtesy of the Oriental Institute, University of Chicago
Copyright © 1998

We define Tradeables™ as either:

1) A set of ideas or actions that help leverage a DEAL without being a part of the deal, or
2) Products and services that satisfy customer needs outside our own product line that are not in competition with our offerings.

Tradeables™ are, in fact, things that create greater negotiation capacity for our own present or future DEALs. Tradeables™ literally means "able" to "trade" or bringing trading capacity. Interestingly, if we extract the word DEAL from Tradeables™, we are left with

Trabes, which in Latin means the beam or the structure of the DEAL.

Many books in the literature teach us about how to get to the best negotiation outcome, the deal within the DEAL. In the making of a DEAL, we must recognize what is negotiable, what is not, and what doesn't need to be negotiated. This is the first step towards securing an optimal outcome. Such simple preparation minimizes wasted resources. However, there are other "things" (Tradeables™) that can make a DEAL happen, even without focusing on the DEAL essence. Here we are proposing an additional tool to get the DEAL from outside the DEAL using Tradeables™.

For example, the essence of a DEAL may be getting someone to provide funds for your new, innovative research ideas. If you have a new research idea or concept, you may want to negotiate with an investor for funds to reduce your ideas to standard business practice. Typically, both the investor and the researcher will focus on acceptable terms. The investor is interested in market value and maximizing return on investment. As a researcher, you may be preoccupied with achieving a target funding level without giving up creative control. The investor wants to get rich; you want to feed both your family and your appetite for creative activities. It could be quite a tug-of-war, as investor and inventor do not speak the same language and come to the table with different objectives stemming from the same potential business arrangement. However, outside the scope of this particular negotiation, the researcher could be developing Tradeables™ with the investor to get both parties closer to a DEAL. Perhaps the researcher could offer to technically evaluate some of the investors other opportunities. Possibly, the researcher could make some contacts for the investor in the patent office. There may be any number of things the researcher could do to build trust for present and future business dealings with this investor.

The primary concept is to seek Tradeables™ in any businesses situation, in addition to understanding our customer's needs, to obtain robust DEALS, rather than mediocre ones. A robust DEAL has the following characteristics:

- A clear vision by both parties,
- Clear objectives, all aligned,
- A cooperative work team,
- A maximum of three visits before closing.

The last trait may seem a bit arbitrary, but minimizing the number of iterations to get mutually agreeable terms is important. Robustness describes both the soundness of the DEAL and the process in its construction. A robust DEAL is one both parties are eager to close and anxious to keep intact.

We have studied different ways to make a DEAL happen and outline the steps of getting to a DEAL, which we will share in Chapter III. However, we have found that even if we follow a trusted negotiation methodology from the literature, we can still get mediocre DEALS if we don't understand the Tradeables™ concept.

We have analyzed multiple highly successful DEALS and found something in common; there are Tradeables™ in all of them, either as ideas or concepts that build trust or as unsolicited "favors" for our customers that help leverage the DEAL. Just as important as trying to describe what Tradeables™ are is recognizing what they are not. Tradeables™ are not "favors" with expectation of one in return. The common saying "I'll scratch your back if you scratch mine" does not apply. Such *quid pro quo* actions do not qualify as Tradeables™. The use of Tradeables™ should never be construed from either side as a bribe. As we shall see, the Phoenician business model is one of openness, fairness, and integrity. It elevates the customer as a long-term business partner ahead of the present DEAL. Any offer outside this framework simply is not in alignment with the spirit of Tradeables™.

DEAL Methodology

We want to examine how Tradeables™ can become standard practice in making a deal, but first we analyze the structure of a deal using the acronym, DEAL.

From the letters in DEAL, we can deduce a simple, yet easy-to-remember, method to obtain a negotiating strategy. The letter D, reminds us that we need to search for the Drivers that help make agreement decisions. The letter E stands for entrapments; find the negotiating barriers on both sides. The letter A challenges us to analyze strengths and weakness of the parties as a cornerstone in a negotiation strategy. The letter L stands for Leverage — what can give us negotiating capacity. Gaining leverage is fundamental to the Tradeables™ concept.

D = Drivers

Some time ago, a client wanted to contract our consulting services. It wasn't a specific motivational need, but an end-of-year tax write off that drove the client decision to hire our services. Sometimes client decisions are perplexing unless we discover the Drivers that really motivate the parties to take the next step.

E = Entrapments

I recall one client's barrier to a DEAL being that the deadline for proposal decision coincided with his daughter's wedding date. The hidden issue was that the client wanted to have a week off to plan the wedding. Without a close relationship with our clients, we can't understand the barriers to the DEAL. We must uncover personal agendas, as well as professional ones. In this instance, the decision was postponed for a month. Foreknowledge of this barrier could have produced an earlier deadline and quicker route to closing the DEAL.

A = Analysis

In our previous book, *DEAL –Guidelines for a Flawless Negotiation*, we proposed the six P's analysis methodology. An ample review of this template for planning and repairing negotiations is provided in the Appendix. In brief, a negotiation is dissected into six elements: Person, Process, Prognosis, Problem, Product, and Power. Analysis can identify a negotiation bottleneck so that a negotiation strategy can be adjusted accordingly. Analysis of the strengths and weaknesses of both parties can help design appropriate strategies to win the DEAL. Knowing the opponent's weakness helps us win the war. Knowing our client's weakness helps us develop better and stronger relationships.

Lack of knowledge, poor preparation, miscommunication, and misunderstanding are among the common weaknesses in negotiating parties. I remember analyzing an important life negotiation with my own methodology and concluded there was no fallback position – no plan B. As a consequence, I didn't rush into closing the DEAL without gathering more information.

As a teenager, I remember requesting permission from my parents to go to the movies or to my friend's house. The answer was consistently a straight, "NO". When I analyzed the situation, I decided a change from question mode to affirmation mode was worth pursuing. Instead of requesting, "Can I go to the movies?" I announced, "I am going to the movies and will be back by 10 o'clock." Exerting this change increased my rate of success to 100%, and merited the response, "Okay, My Son, be careful."

Analyzing the other party is essential in getting them to agree to your requests. Know their strengths and weakness, likes and dislikes, and you have an inside track to a DEAL.

Finally,

L = Leverage

This is the best kept secret of ancient Phoenician negotiators, the *Traders of the Sea*. Tradeables™ give leverage and negotiation capacity. However, many things can create leverage in a negotiation that are not Tradeables™. Let's us illustrate this point with the following anecdote.

A formerly married couple requested a favor of me. They were having difficulties communicating their needs and wants directly following the separation. I was enlisted to be a mediator to help them sort through their difficult situation in the aftermath of their divorce. In order to help them, I first had to learn their needs and wants. Analyzing my friends' case enabled me to create a series of strategies to get from A to Z in their particular negotiation process. The first strategy was to agree upon a time frame long enough to achieve a win-win scenario with multiple options to satisfy their needs. Their kids' well-being was set as a top priority in the negotiating strategy.

In this case, I had significant leverage on the negotiation, because I knew both ex-husband and ex-wife since childhood, and they both trusted me to handle their difficult situation. They both respected me as an objective and collaborative friend. Trust and respect, however, are not Tradeables™, though they supplied ample leverage to sort their differences amicably.

While trust and respect are not Tradeables™, they often are the result of using the practice of Tradeables™ in routine business transactions. Negotiations using Tradeables™ are time-tested means to produce long-term business relationships and return customers. Let's step back in time to see Tradeables™ at work in the ancient culture of the Phoenicians, the *Master Traders of the Sea*.

The whole cannot be well unless the parts are well.
–Plato

Chapter II. The Ancient Art of Negotiation

The Cedars Destined for the Temple: Gustave Doré, Bible illustrator

Ancient Negotiating Masters

The idea behind Tradeables™ was practiced by the best known negotiators and traders of human history, the Phoenicians. In "*Phoenicians: Lebanon's Epic Heritage*", historian Sanford Holst mentions the seven principles of the Phoenician society that helped them survive as a culture for centuries, while whole nations and surrounding people groups perished. These same seven principles were interwoven into a negotiation style that established the Phoenicians as the premiere trading culture and the business partner of choice. We discuss these principles, with the author's permission, in this book, *Negotiate Like a Phoenician* – dedicated to the greatest traders ever, the Phoenicians.

Three words of caution:

- First, by no means have we intended this to be either a history book or a religious book. Our intent is to bring several passages of history from the Phoenicians negotiating philosophy and principles to our modern world, day-to-day negotiation scenarios.

- Second, in every society there is good and evil. Here, we are pointing out the good and best of the Phoenician society. No doubt, there was also bad in their society. This is not a commentary on social mores. We are solely interested in their best business and negotiating practices.

- Third, we quote from the Bible as a primary source document of scripts between Phoenicians and other cultures with which they were negotiating. By no means is the intent of this book to bring religious discussion to the readers. It is only a source of information backing up our negotiating research.

Who Were the Phoenicians?

The Phoenicians were Canaanites, who rose to prominence in the second millennia BCE, with no particular cultural distinction from their neighbors except they were guardians of a great natural resource, cedar. Everyone came to them for wood, so they adopted a merchant lifestyle. The Phoenicians had a great product, but in a region of kings and conflicts, how could they avoid the crosshairs of conquering nations? The answer lies partly in diversification. The Phoenicians made themselves valuable in the eyes of their neighbors with an array of goods and services they alone could bring to the table. They were able to convince their neighbors to buy rather than conquer based on the perception that a long-term business relationship was in everyone's best interest.

In *The Histories* (Rawlinson, 1997), Herodotus (I.1) describes the Phoenicians from Persian accounts.

[The Phoenicians], who had formerly dwelt on the shores of the Erythraean Sea, having migrated to the Mediterranean and settled in the parts which they now inhabit, began at once, they say, to adventure on long voyages, freighting their vessels with the wares of Egypt and Assyria. They landed at many places on the coast, and among the rest at Argos, which was then pre-eminent above all the states included now under the common name of Hellas (p. 5).

In this passage, the Erythraean Sea is not the modern Red Sea but rather " ... *that sea into which the Euphrates, a river broad, deep, and rapid, flows* (Herodotus, I.180)." Herodotus thus gives us history, geography, and noted occupation as sea merchants. The Phoenicians were not just local traders but embarked on long voyages – the first "business road warriors," except their road was no road at all.

Several authors (Johnston, 1965; Herm, 1975, Moscati, 1968) contend that the Phoenicians were a blended people of the early Canaanite settlers on the coast of Syria and the Hyksos people forced from Egypt around 1200 BCE. Herm (1975) places the expulsion of the Hyksos from the delta of Egypt coincident with the enslavement of the house of Joseph and sons of Jacob in Hebrew history. On the other hand, Johnston claims the exodus occurred about the time of Abraham.

Regardless, the Hyksos, or Shepherd Kings, migrated to Egypt and remained some 600 years, absorbing much of that culture, especially in terms of science, mathematics, and art. The Hyksos are recorded in history as aggressors, since they destroyed temples and killed in the process. Herodotus, however, suggests these actions were out of religious fervor – an attempt to rid the land of the animal worship that had become pervasive in ancient Egypt. Regardless, when powerful enough, Egyptian armies forced a mass exodus. As cited by Johnston (1965), Manetho, Egyptian historian wrote,

> *They agreed to evacuate the fortress on condition that they should be permitted to leave the country, and, by virtue of this agreement, they withdrew from Egypt with all their families and possessions, to the number of 240,000 men, and traversed the desert into Syria. Fearing, however, the power of the Assyrians, who were masters of Asia, they turned into Palestine and in that past which is now called Judea built a city which should be sufficient for so large a number of men, and called it Jerusalem.*

The Hyksos found a new home across the sea in those Canaanite coastal regions. The influx brought knowledge and interest in developing business beyond the natural resources of the region. Tyre and Sidon were certainly already established, but the arrival of the Hyksos marked a shift in lifestyle from simple traders toward manufacturing, as well as defining Phoenicia proper.

There is a great drive to physically locate the center of Phoenician society. As such, the coastal region is recognized as the ancestral home, but the Phoenician coastal ports were little more than a hub of operations. The Phoenicians are rightly associated with the sea, and they colonized ports wherever their business took them. This philosophy of expansion is one reason the Phoenicians had such profound influence on neighboring people groups. It is also a reason we simply cannot call the cities of Byblos, Tyre, and Sidon, plus a handful of smaller villages, as Phoenicia. These cities, though important, were only loosely drawn into confederation. The cities were, for most of recorded history, autonomous with separate kings. Sometimes they acted in alliance; sometimes they acted in defiance. On this note, Moscati (1979) stated, *"On the whole the names which designate the Phoenicians as a unity are rarely used, at least as far as the Phoenicians themselves are concerned, and this stresses the division of the area and the prevalence of city consciousness over national consciousness."*

In a period of enormous regional conflict, who will conquer the Phoenicians? As a dispersed population of sea-going people, they were neither accessible to land-based armies nor an easy target for any foe without a comparable fleet. In the time period, there were none.

The Phoenician Business Model

The basic business model of the ancient Phoenicians is captured in a quote from Johnston (1965).

The mere fact that the main trend of the business of the Phoenicians was always toward the great centres of civilization, makes it apparent that it was not only on account of the quality of their goods but equally on account of their manner of disposing of them that they were highly approved. There is, nevertheless, just as little doubt that while the transactions of the larger merchants in the great centres of population such as Babylonia, Yemen, Greece, and Egypt earned for the Phoenicians a reputation for probity and trustworthiness, the commerce of the outlying regions and the more sparsely populated territories opened up by the increasing radius of their navigation was largely in the hands of bold and often unscrupulous adventurers. Still it is difficult to conceive of business being continued on such lines much beyond the incipient stages …It is, therefore, more than probable that after a few generations the traders with the main centres of civilization must have recognized that a continuously profitable business could only be conducted by a practical application of the belief that honesty was the best policy (p. 74).

The Phoenicians knew the value of a good location, and they established many such centrally-located staging areas between the major market centers of Babylon, Egypt, Arabia, and along the Mediterranean coast. The Phoenicians were preoccupied with growing the business and their supply network.

The Phoenicians had a solid base of raw materials from which to work.

- Cedar – Wood was a valuable commodity in the region, and little was to be found anywhere but in the forests of Lebanon. Fragrant cedar became the product of choice for building projects from ships to temples.

- Dyes – The Phoenicians learned to extract red, blue, and especially violet dyes from sea snails and mollusks. They recognized the market value of this prized product and understood their customer. The Phoenicians supplied the deep purple dyes to an elitist market – kings and royalty. The very name "Phoenicians" is derived from the Greek word for purple. In reference to themselves, they were Canaanites; to their customers, they were Phoenicians.

- Transportation – From their own cedar, the Phoenicians made sailing vessels, enabling them to expand their markets and their product lines. The Phoenicians had merchant ships for cargo and fast, sleek ships as security convoys. They set up trading posts throughout the region and created a network of hubs, extending the range of trading missions. The Phoenicians were explorers. They were not content with the status quo when it came to business. Their trading posts allowed them to probe the outlying regions for other marketable products. As a result, the Phoenicians became purveyors of Spanish silver, copper, and tin. They marketed African ivory and baboons. Of course, they ferried vast quantities of gold. Later, the Phoenicians hired out their vessels and crews to other nations for both military and commercial use.

The Phoenicians leveraged their timber, dye, and shipping knowledge into a trading empire without equal.

Concerning the markets of Babylon and Arabia, the Phoenicians competed with land-based caravans for delivery of similar goods. Sea-based transportation simply was in a different time-to-market class, enabling more rapid turnaround and higher trading capacity. The Phoenician practice of setting up ports where land-based goods could be easily staged and uploaded for transport proved beneficial for all parties. Rather than compete with a business with a similar product line, the Phoenicians simply turned that competitor into a business partner, adding his strength to their arsenal.

While coinage was issued in later times, the early Phoenician mercantile system was one of barter. As such, nearly every transaction was a negotiation. With the standard practice of establishing fixed position trading posts with easy sea access, the Phoenicians were bent on return business and long-term trading partnerships. Thus, they dealt fairly with customers, knowing the value of the goods of origin and the market demand for those goods.

Concerning the desire for expansion of their product line, Harden (1962, p.137) states, *"The Phoenicians, energetic as they were, and with a good bent for money-making, soon learnt to develop industries of their own, based first on the raw materials which their land and coastal waters provided, but later on imported raw materials as well."*

The Phoenicians, thus, adopted the business philosophy:

- ☑ Have a solid product base
- ☑ Locate centrally
- ☑ Expand geographically
- ☑ Grow inventory
- ☑ Fill commodity and retail markets
- ☑ Price fairly
- ☑ Deal honestly
- ☑ Deliver the goods

Using sea transport, the Phoenicians were able to supply both raw and finished goods more readily from all known corners of the world at a fair price to the return customer.

TraDEAbLes™

Leveraging Business via Technology

Communication

With all the pomp and circumstance around sailing technology, manufacturing, and sea trade, one can easily lose sight of perhaps the single most important advancement owed to the Phoenician people – the alphabet. The Phoenicians developed a 22-letter alphabet which replaced older pictorial forms of written communication.

Surprisingly, little Phoenician writing from within their own culture has survived. What we know of the Phoenicians is documented in external accounts of history, such as those of Pliny, Josephus, Herodotus and others. It's not that the Phoenicians did not document, for historical records speak otherwise. However, we have only indirect quoting from the annals of Tyre by writers such as Josephus. It has been suggested that only the extensive writing and recordkeeping of the Phoenicians enabled them to manage their fleets of magnificent trading vessels, track inventory in their extensive network of trading posts, and schedule the deliveries of raw products and finished goods to the markets of the known world (Film Ideas, 2003).

Construction

While some of the artistic undertakings by the Phoenicians were of such grand scale to qualify as construction projects, here we site one of the more overlooked technologies of the Phoenicians, land-based engineering. Under Egyptian King Necho, the Phoenicians were pivotal in attempts to construct the first Suez canal, connecting Mediterranean and Red Sea. It was during this construction effort in 611 BCE that a complementary exploration effort, the circumnavigation of the African continent, was commissioned of the Phoenicians as recorded by Herodotus (IV. 42).

As we shall see, the Phoenicians were instrumental in the construction of the Hebrew temple for Solomon, but Moscati (1968) notes that Phoenicians from Tyre and Sidon were employed in building the palace of Nimrud under Assurnasirpal II as well. The Phoenicians were guardians of the forests of Lebanon, supplying wood for many such projects, but their services and expertise went far beyond the mere felling of trees and hauling of timber.

Shipbuilding

The Phoenicians were master shipbuilders. Many artist renderings of Phoenician vessels looking little more than multi-paddle canoes do them a grievous disservice. Josephus traveled the seas aboard a ship carrying 600 passengers in the first century. The ship capacity described in the Pauline letters is comparable to modern grain ships. The Phoenicians built ships according to need. They had massive cargo vessels and fast security fleets. The port at Carthage is estimated to have housed 200 ships (Film Ideas, 2003). Johnston (1965) records a detailed description of an armed merchant ship by Xenophon (Oecon., VIII. ii) around 500 BCE.

> *I think that one of the best and most perfect arrangements of things that I ever saw was when I went to look at the great Phoenician sailing vessels, for I saw there the largest amount of naval tacking separately disposed in the smallest stowage.*

He went on to describe an incredible use of space for a crew predisposed to haul goods, ride out a storm, or defend the ship and cargo. The primary point is that the Phoenicians developed and implemented technology necessary to support their business. Their ambitious business aspirations drove them to press the envelope of technology to preserve operations and their standings as master merchants of the sea.

Navigation

On the subject of navigation, there is wide opinion. Moscati (1968) summarized the maritime exploits of the Phoenicians as cautious and limited. He writes:

> *For lack of compass, navigation was performed under the guidance of Ursa Minor, which the Greeks called 'Phoenician'. The ships did not go far out to sea: the Phoenicians, as we shall see in the chapter on their Mediterranean expansion, probably founded their landing-stages at a day's voyage apart, so as to be able to shelter on the*

mainland at night. Nevertheless, they were not deterred by the most distant destinations and made special use of the islands as anchorages in the open sea. (p. 87)

In counterpoint, Johnston (1965) makes a compelling argument, thoroughly backed by research and documentation, that the Phoenicians held all the technology necessary to support voyages to the Americas.

There are points which are not in contention. While the Persian Gulf was easily navigated, the Mediterranean was complex, requiring knowledge of seasonal weather patterns and ships capable of riding out fierce storms. As far as navigation goes, the Phoenicians are credited with the recognition of the North or Pole Star as a constant in the skies. As already seen, some even refer to it as '*The Phoenician*'. Johnston cites Strabo (XVI. 757) on Phoenician use of arithmetic correction on steering in night navigation. Herodotus (III. 136) also refers to Phoenician navigational charting of coastlands. Thus, the Phoenicians had sturdy ships and capability to navigate by day and a clear night sky. The only necessary navigational technology in dispute was the compass. Regardless, the Phoenicians had technology to conduct more than mere coasting voyages.

Manufacturing

The Phoenicians added manufacturing capacity to their base of raw materials. The Hyksos brought to Phoenician culture weaving (linen), stone masonry, pyramid construction, pottery, and gemstone engraving skills from Egypt. The Phoenicians supplied metal goods from the converted raw materials of gold, silver, tin, etc. brought from world markets. They not only dealt in purple dye, but they manufactured wool and linen end-products. The Phoenicians were the first craftsmen to make and supply clear glass made from regional sand of high purity. No, the Phoenicians were not simply purveyors of raw materials; they developed the capacity to bring finished goods into the marketplace, covering the commodity and retail markets.

Mining

While we are unaware of the technological advances of the Phoenicians with respect to the act of mining, we know that the Phoenicians were in constant search of ores of all sorts. Herodotus (VI. 47) says,

> *I myself have seen the [gold] mines in questions: by far the most curious of them are those which the Phoenicians discovered at the time when they went with Thasus and colonized the island, which afterwards took its name from him. These Phoenician workings are in Thasos itself, between Coenyra and a place called AEnyra, over against Samothrace. A huge mountain has been turned*

upside down in the search of ores. Such then was the source of their wealth. (The Histories, p.462)

Metals and mining also spurred an interest in Phoenician exploration. Of particular interest is the region of Ophir, intimately associated with gold. While common thought equates Ophir to Yemen, there is ample reason for speculation. According to Hebrew history, Ophir was a grandson of Noah, and the name probably was associated with the region settled by him and his descendents along the Indian Ocean on the Arabian peninsula. Josephus (Jewish Antiquities, Book 1, Chapter 6 4(147)) recorded, *"Now Joktan, one of the sons of Eber, had these sons, Almodad, Sheleph, Hazarmaveth, Jerah, Hadoram, Uzal, Diklah, Obal, Abimael, Sheba, Ophir, Havilah, and Jobab. These inhabited from Cophen, an Indian River, and in part of Asia adjoining to it."* Still, was there enough gold in this region to supply the quantities cited as delivered by Phoenician trading voyages?

A similar quandary is conjured by the term, *ships of Tarshish,* which we shall encounter in examination of ancient negotiation scripts. Vast quantities of silver are associated with Tarshish, usually assigned to Spain. The name is similar to that of a son of Javan, who settled in Southern Italy. It is proposed that rather than a distinct place, Tarshish referred to a distant settlement boundary. If so, the name association pushed westward with expansion. If this interpretation is correct, ships of Tarshish were simply vessels capable of long voyages to the edge of known settlement.

With the Phoenician practice of colonization, a land rich in metal ores was reason enough to establish an outpost or a series of outposts to support mining operations and the transport of those goods. Consequently, mining was motivation for exploration.

Exploration

Trade expansion, the nature of business, and locale of raw materials and ports demanded advancement in shipbuilding and navigation, but the desire for new products, faster routes, and additional sources for raw materials drove the Phoenicians beyond the Mediterranean. The Phoenicians are known to have traveled to Britain for tin and set up ports on the western coast of Africa. The account of circumnavigation of Africa also cannot be discounted.

No one, however, argues so exhaustively and persuasively as Johnston (1965) for the role of the Phoenicians as explorers. In his book, *Did the Phoenicians discover America?*, Johnston claims that the Phoenicians did just that, leaving a trail throughout the Pacific. As a simple example, cotton, which Herodotus claims as native to India, is traceable through the Pacific Islands to America.

Johnston claims that the Phoenician, Hebrew, Thracian, and Scythian cultures, those most likely represented on Phoenician vessel crews, are present in a chain of unlikely 'coincidences' from the Bahrein Islands to Ceylon to Golden Chersonese to Java to the

Torres Straits to the Caroline Islands to Tonga to Samoa to Rappa to Tahiti to Easter Island to America – the proposed route to Ophir aboard the very ships of Tarshish commissioned by King Hiram of Tyre and King Solomon of Israel. Such were three-year voyages on a fleet built and launched from Ezion Geber on the Red Sea, not on the Mediterranean. In I Kings 9, it says,

> *26 King Solomon also built ships at Ezion Geber, which is near Elath in Edom, on the shore of the Red Sea.*
>
> *27 And Hiram sent his men – sailors who knew the sea – to serve in the fleet with Solomon's men.*
>
> *28 They sailed to Ophir and brought back 420 talents of gold, which they delivered to King Solomon.*

2 Chronicles 8 offers a little more detail on the role of the Phoenicians as shipbuilders of this fleet.

> *17 Then Solomon went to Ezion Geber and Elath on the coast of Edom.*
>
> *18 And Hiram sent him ships commanded by his own officers, men who knew the sea. These, with Solomon's men, sailed to Ophir and brought back four hundred and fifty talents of gold, which they delivered to King Solomon.*

TraDEAbLes™

Fleets launched from Ezion Geber would not likely be headed for Spain. King Jehoshaphat constructed another fleet at Ezion Geber generations later, but that flotilla never took sail.

The itemized primary cargo delivered is also provided to us.

2 Chronicles 9

> *21 The king had a fleet of trading ships [of Tarshısh] manned by Hiram's men. Once every three years it returned, carrying gold, silver and ivory, and apes and baboons [or peacocks].*

Indeed, the cargo list's inclusion of peacocks would point to eastward travel through Sumatra, the natural habitat of the flamboyant bird. Johnston argues that the remainder of the cargo list simply could not be accomplished by known colonies along this route. Tracing further along the likely final bearing simply brings into record a number of other plausible landing sites with mysterious Mediterranean-like names, symbols, customs, and folklore. Only until the Americas are reached is the cargo bill possibly filled.

Johnston argues that the Phoenicians had a crude compass in either loadstone or bactellium form to round out the list of essentials needed for establishing and following trade routes across the Pacific. While the cities of Tyre and Sidon were of extreme importance, Johnston (1965) cites the Phoenician colonies on the Bahrein Islands as a central hub of operations. Their presence there was confirmed by Pliny and Strabo. The Bahrein Islands provided a link between Arabian and Babylonian markets. Sea trade could be accomplished at a fraction of cost of land-based caravans covering the same markets. However, just as the Phoenicians ventured westward out of the Mediterranean, the Bahrein Islands offered a launch point for comparable voyages to the east.

When European explorers reached the New World, they found it already colonized with what experts say were non-indigenous people. In many ways, these native people had in their possession advanced technology which would have resided with the Phoenicians. Johnston claims the mystery of the Piedra de Agua, or Water Stone – with its ancient compass markings, could be explained by such Phoenician exploration, as could countless other symbols and legends associated with Aztec, Incan, and Mayan civilizations. Certainly, the ores of Mexico could have made 'silver as common as stones' in Solomon's time. Indeed, Johnston strings together a compelling argument of well-researched facts and inferences which led him to conclude that the Phoenicians with their Hebrew partners and mercenary crews of Scythians and Thracians reached the Americas with the fleets commissioned by Solomon and Hiram. After the decline of Phoenician dominance, these colonies would have been isolated until European expeditions centuries later.

TraDEAbLes™

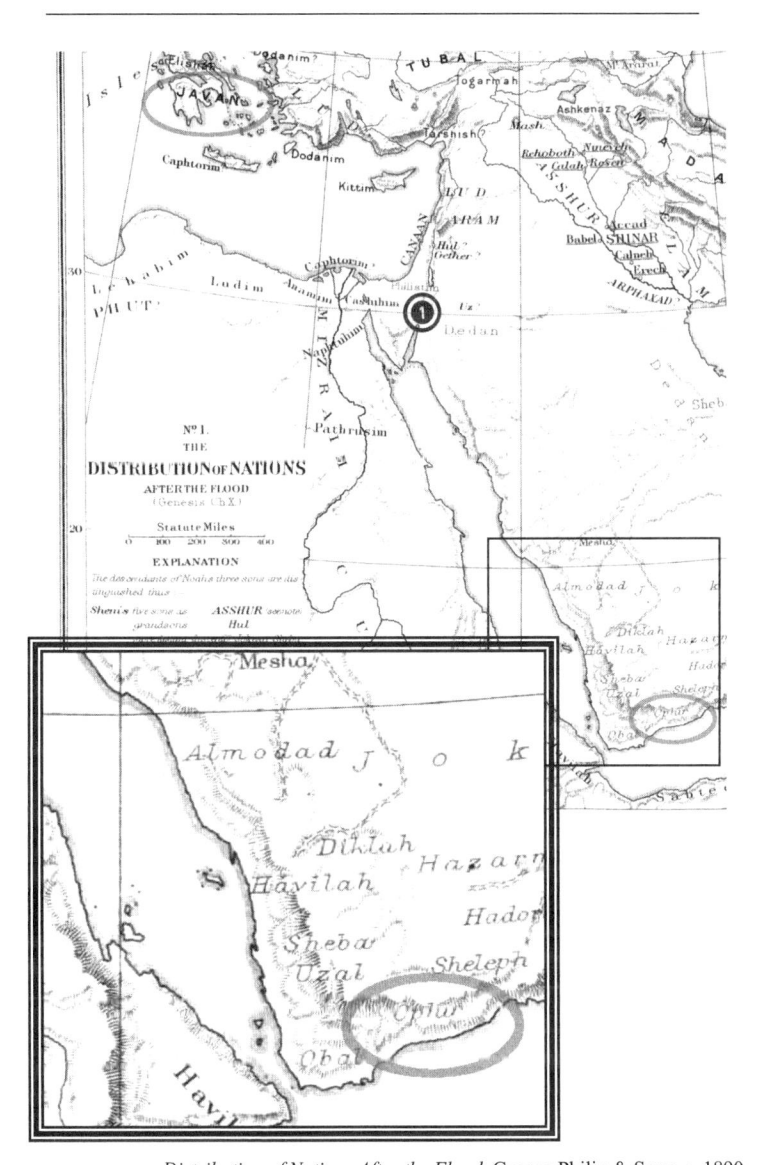

Distribution of Nations After the Flood, George Philip & Sons, c. 1890
Bible Atlas, Plate I, Society for Promoting Christian Knowledge, London
Note: Regions of interest highlighted include settled areas of Javan and Ophir
① indicates the city of Ezion Geber, the launch point for fleets of Hiram & Solomon

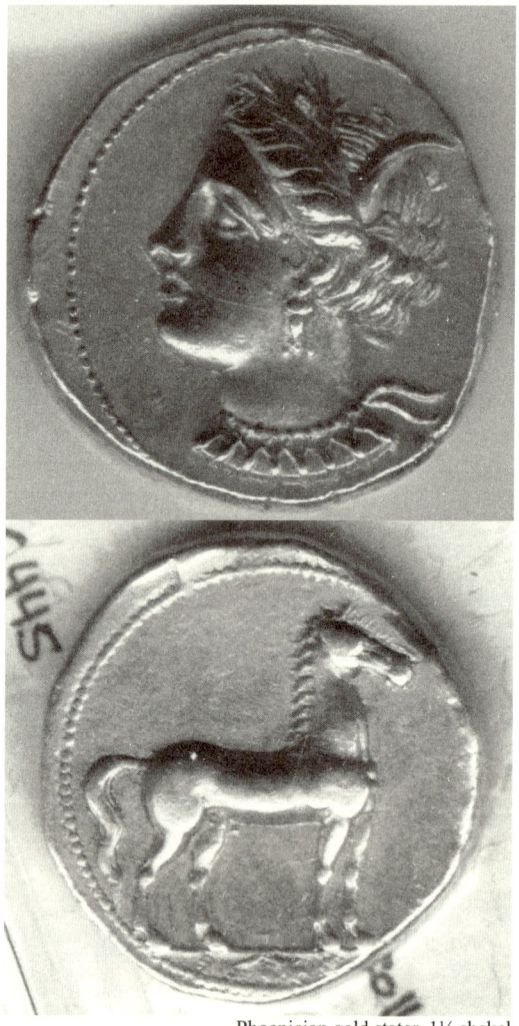

Phoenician gold stater, 1¼ shekel
Carthage mint, c. 341 BCE
Obverse: Wreathed head of Tanit
Reverse: Punic horse with what some scholars believe is a map of the ancient world in the exergue area beneath the horse, supporting the Phoenician discovery of the Americas; Jenkins-Lewis 9, same dies
Photos by Mark McMenamin

War

While we highlight the Phoenician preference for peaceful resolution of differences, there was always need to protect trading routes and valuable cargoes. If required, however, the Phoenicians were found to be admirable foes in armed conflict, as experienced by the Babylonian invaders of Nebuchadnezzar, the Macedonian armies of Alexander the Great, and the Romans facing the likes of Hannibal in the Punic Wars.

Henri-Paul Motte, circa 1880s engravings
Hannibal Crosses the Rhone (left) and *unknown title* (right)

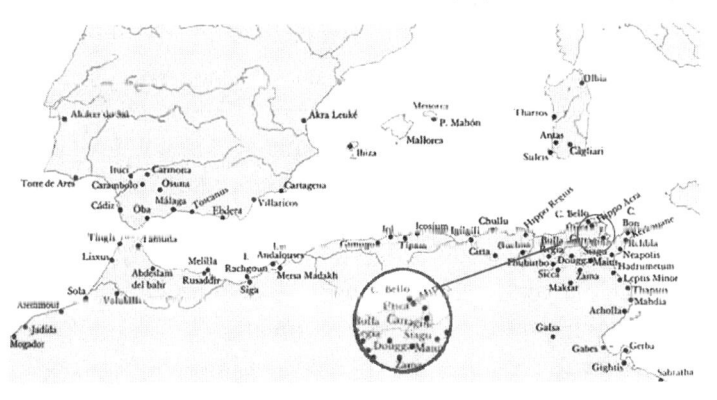

Map of the Ancient Mediterranean, Marcos Arana Cervantes
in *Ramas del Mismo Cedro*, 2006, p. 27; inset shows Carthage region
Courtesy of Centro México Libanés de Guadalajara

Phoenician Cultural Survival

Following 400 years of slavery, when the Israelites came out of Egypt after the 10 plagues, Moses led them to their promised land, Canaan – the land of inheritance for Abraham's descendents. The only problem was that the land was occupied. To avoid corruption of their religion, the Israelites were to forcibly displace all people from the region. Army after army fell without survivor. The Phoenicians, however, remained and thrived as a culture. When Israel peaked in regional political dominance, so did the Phoenicians in terms of commerce. Israel had the wealth, and the Phoenicians had the goods. The Phoenicians remained a vibrant society until the invasion of King Nebuchadnezzar in 573 BCE forced a retreat from the old city of Tyre. The island fortress remained a stronghold until the conquest of Alexander the Great in 332 BCE. The center of Phoenician culture then dissipated to the numerous colonies along the Mediterranean and the coast of Africa, such as Carthage.

The Phoenicians were guardians of great products, serving well-cultivated and niche markets. They positioned themselves as trading partners of choice with a diverse product base and services, but goods without salesmanship is not a working combination. The Phoenicians were great communicators. They created the phonetic alphabet that placed reading and writing in the hands of the masses. This was a great equalizer in their society, as education and the written record were not elitist privileges of only kings, priests, and scribes.

TraDEAbLes™

According to Sanford Holst,

> *The Phoenicians did not become outstanding negotiators by calculation or contrivance, but simply out of necessity. They did what was necessary to survive, and then to thrive. The principles presented in "Phoenicians: Lebanon's Epic Heritage" guided their society, but also guided their business. Their business was the negotiation of trade and the transport of goods by sea in their sturdy boats of Lebanese cedar. Because of their principles, they became the master sea-traders of their day, and continued to flourish for three thousand years.*

The 7 Principles of the Best Negotiators Ever

1) Create partnerships
2) Trade internationally
3) Resolve differences peacefully
4) Express religious tolerance
5) Respect women
6) Uphold equality
7) Retain Privacy

Let's examine each of these principles and then look at some case studies of business dealings of this ancient culture.

1) Create partnerships
   Sanford Holst says, "Too many people look for the quick profit, or the trade which harms the person with whom they are trading. By contrast, the Phoenician principles caused these savvy traders to not only take profit for themselves, but always leave their trading partner with some benefit as well. This ensured the Phoenicians' long-term survival and success, because their trading partner was motivated to return to them for more trade – and the additional benefit which came with it." The Phoenicians wanted return business. They pursued long-term relationships. The Phoenicians also chose their partnerships wisely, allying with power and sensing shifts in it. Holst also notes, "When the deals were done, the Phoenicians were able to enjoy the rich benefits with their partners within the community, with their women, and in peace."

2) Trade internationally
   The Phoenicians permeated the market. Wherever the products and market existed, they went. As savvy sea traders, they had access to an unparalleled network of clients and goods, and they could link the two.

TraDEAbLes™

3) <u>Resolve differences peacefully</u>
The Phoenicians' business was business, avoiding the snares of political alliances that can bring down societies with their allies.

4) <u>Express religious tolerance</u>
The Phoenicians did business with cultures with vastly different religious beliefs. Their own religious practices did not interfere with their desire or ability to conduct business. At the same time, they were quite knowledgeable of the religious drivers of their clients. Still, religious tolerance does not mean a willingness to compromise values – a practice never advocated.

5) <u>Respect women</u>
According to Holst, "Respect for women not only allowed these members of the community to contribute in a positive manner, but also allowed the Phoenicians to reach beneficial agreements which others refused to consider." Women were (are) half the market, and they widen the product need base. This respect for women in their own society probably helped them meet client needs, as they would not ignore the market force of women, despite a lack of political power in most ancient cultures with whom they dealt.

6) <u>Uphold equality</u>
While the Phoenicians did have a monarchy, according to Holst, "Equality among the Phoenicians enabled them to avoid disputes among themselves, and to channel all their energy and abilities to dealing with others."

7) <u>Retain privacy</u>
Interestingly, Holst makes a keen observation concerning negotiating power when he says, "The privacy of their internal affairs likewise was a strong negotiating lever, for it denied to the person on the other side of the table the ability to take advantage."

The way the Phoenicians approached business is, in essence, the Tradeables™ spirit – taking business practice far beyond the mere aspects of getting the DEAL. If we practice at least the seven principles of the ancient Phoenicians, we can increase our chances of finding Tradeables™ in any given DEAL.

Good sense, not age, brings wisdom
Syrus, Maxims

TraDEAbLes™

Case Studies from Ancient Historians

La Stele di Nora, Sardina, c. 8th century BCE
Courtesy of Salvatore Dedòla; http://www.linguasarda.com
Currently in Museo Archeologico Nazionale, Napoli

Get it in Writing

In *Against Apion* I.17.107, the words of Josephus, first century Jewish historian, concerning the record-keeping practice of the Phoenicians of Tyre are translated by Whiston (1999).

> *There are then records among the Tyrians that take in the history of many years, and these are public writings, and are kept with great exactness, and include accounts of the facts done among them, and such as concern their transactions with other nations also, those I mean which were worth remembering* (p.943).

This passage reveals the Phoenicians to document thoroughly and publicly both matters of record and business dealings.

In VIII.2.8.55, Josephus again wrote on the authenticity and preservation of historical business records. In this instance, he spoke of the specific letter exchange between the king of Tyre and Solomon, king of Israel, which we shall discuss in detail in forthcoming sections. Josephus recorded,

> *The copies of these letters remain to this day, and are preserved not only in our books, but among the Tyrians also; insomuch that if anyone would know the certainty about them, he may desire the keepers of the public records of Tyre to show him them, and he will find what is there set down to agree with what we have said* (p. 270).

The Phoenician people were empowered enough to have personal correspondence between monarchs available for public inspection. Terms and conditions were clear, written, and open to inspection. This speaks much toward the principle of equality, even in the shadow of monarchial practice.

A Policy of Tribute

Tradeables™ can include tribute, or unsolicited gifting. Often in history, we find the Phoenicians weighing the consequences of resistance and deciding in favor of preservation of life and business. As an example, the Assyrians were notoriously ruthless and periodically invaded the Phoenician coast. The Phoenicians repeatedly used a policy of appeasement. In roughly 875 BCE, the annals of Tiglatpileser I (ARAB: I. 479) record,

> *At that time I marched along the side of Mount Lebanon, and to the Great Sea of the land of Amurru I went up. In the Great Sea I washed my weapons, and I made offerings unto the gods. The tribute of the kings of the seacoast, of the people of Tyre, Sidon, Byblos, Makhalata, Maisa, Kaisa, Amurru, and Aradus, which lies in the midst of the sea, -- silver, gold, lead, copper, vessels of bronze, garments made of brightly coloured wool, linen garments, a great monkey, and a small monkey, maple-wood, boxwood, and ivory, and a nahiru [dolphin], a creature of the sea, I received as tribute from them, and they embraced my feet.*

Moscati (1968) adds, "*The Phoenician cities do not seem to offer any armed resistance, and there is no mention of battle. This would be in character with the traditional policy of the small states, which preferred to satisfy their powerful neighbors with homages and tributes* (p.16)." If Phoenicians gave gifts, they could regain their loss. These tributes pre-empted actions that would be more costly in the long term. Especially when dealing with the Assyrians, the Phoenicians made liberal use of Tradeables™ in the form of unsolicited tribute.

A Good Reputation

The Phoenicians

> *Upon the Erythrean sea the people live*
> *Who style themselves Phoenicians.*
> *These are sprung from the true Erythrean stock,*
> *From the sage race, who first essayed the deep,*
> *And wafted merchandise to coasts unknown.*
> *These too, digested first the starry choir,*
> *Their motions marked, and called them by their name.*
> Dionysius – Pliny, v. 965.

This short poem tells us a great deal about the Phoenicians. First, we are given the geography of operations – the Erythrean Sea. The Phoenicians are called a sage race who knew the oceans and were among the first road warrior class of businessmen who traveled upon their ships to unknown places. They not only knew the sea, but the Phoenicians mapped the night sky, no doubt for navigation. This poem casts a favorable light on the people "who style themselves Phoenicians."

TraDEAbLes™

First Contact Sales or Silent Negotiation

Herodotus (IV. 196) describes a typical first contact sales approach practiced by the Phoenicians.

The Carthaginians also relate the following: -- There is a country in Libya, and a nation, beyond the Pillars of Heracles, which they are wont to visit, where they no sooner arrive but forthwith they unlade their wares, and, having disposed them after an orderly fashion along the beach, leave them, and, returning aboard their ships, raise a great smoke. The natives, when they see the smoke, come down to the shore, and laying out to view so much gold as they think the worth of the wares, withdraw to a distance. The Carthaginians upon this come ashore and look. If they think the gold enough, they take it and go their way; but if it does not seem to them sufficient, they go aboard ship once more, and wait patiently. Then the others approach and add to their gold, till the Carthaginians are content. Neither party deals unfairly by the other: for they themselves never touch the gold till it comes up to the worth of their goods, nor do the natives ever carry off the goods till the gold is taken away (The Histories, p. 381-2).

Here we see a most probable example of a cross-cultural negotiation that is both respectful and equitable. The Phoenicians must have developed extensive skill in communication without complete knowledge of their trading partner's native language.

As this account comes from the Carthaginian era, trades were no doubt brokered in gold as opposed to pure barter. The cited Pillars of Heracles is the ancient name for the Straits of Gibraltar. Herm (1975) adds, "*In this way the first contacts were made. A counter-offer followed the first offering, and then the silent bargaining began, needing much tact, inventiveness and also honesty. The merchants did not want to spoil a possible new market before they had begun, a feeling apparently appreciated by their customers.*" Whether first contact or not, the Phoenician customer was dealt fairly.

Standing on Principles

The Phoenicians coveted peace and mutual prosperity, but at times, they were compelled to fight for their preservation. In the *Life and Works of Flavius Josephus* (Antiquities: IX. xiv), we see a time when Assyrian aggression required physical reprisal. Initially, we see that not only Phoenicia was in Assyrian crosshairs.

> 1. When Shalmaneser, the king of Assyria, had it told him, that [Hoshea] the king of Israel had sent privately to So, the king of Egypt, desiring his assistance against him, he was very angry, and made an expedition against Samaria, in the seventh year of the reign of Hoshea; but when he was not admitted [into the city] by the king, he besieged Samaria three years, and took it by force in the ninth year of the reign of Hoshea, and in the seventh year of Hezekiah,

TraDEAbLes™

king of Jerusalem, and quite demolished the government of the Israelites, and transplanted all the people into Media and Persia, among whom he took king Hoshea alive; and when he had removed these people out of this their land, he transplanted other nations out of Cuthah, a place so called, (for there is [still] a river of that name in Persia,) into Samaria, and into the country of the Israelites. ...

2. *And now the king of Assyria invaded all Syria and Phoenicia in a hostile manner. The name of this king is also set down in the archives of Tyre, for he made an expedition against Tyre in the reign of Eluleus; and Menander attests to it, who, when he wrote his Chronology, and translated the archives of Tyre into the Greek language, gives us the following history: "One whose name was Eluleus reigned thirty-six years; this king, upon the revolt of the Citteans, sailed to them, and reduced them to a submission. Against these did the king of Assyria send an army, and in a hostile manner overrun all Phoenicia, but soon made peace with them all, and returned back; but Sidon, and Ace, and Palaetyrus revolted; and many other cities there were which delivered themselves up to the king of Assyria. Accordingly, when the Tyrians would not submit to him, the king returned, and fell upon them again, while the Phoenicians had furnished him with threescore ships, and eight hundred men to row them; and when the*

> *Tyrians had come upon them in twelve ships, and the enemy's ships were dispersed, they took five hundred men prisoners, and the reputation of all the citizens of Tyre was thereby increased; but the king of Assyria returned, and placed guard at their rivers and aqueducts, who should hinder the Tyrians from drawing water. This continued for five years; and still the Tyrians bore the siege, and drank of the water they had out of the wells they dug." And this is what is written in the Tyrian archives concerning Shalmaneser, the king of Assyria.*

Phoenicians first sought peace and attained it, but that solution was short-lived. The Tyrians were hold-outs to submission, and they showed their steel by defeating a much larger navy equipped with their own ships. When confronted with tactics meant to drive them from their stronghold, the Tyrians improvised and outlasted the opposition. The reputation of Tyrians increased greatly throughout the region because of their stance and the ability to resist a notorious regional aggressor.

The island fortress of Tyre was a persistent reminder of the strength of Phoenician will. While the Assyrians and Nebuchadnezzar found little land-based resistance, the Tyrian fortress proved too impervious to their military conquests. This was the case until Alexander the Great determined to take Tyre at any cost. In the *Greek Historians* (Godolphin, 1942), we have from the writings of Arrian (Anabasis: II. 15-24) a detailed account of Alexander's assault on Tyre and the ingenious countermeasures by the Tyrians to prolong the taking of the island fortress against enormous resources. Despite the massive construction of a land bridge by invading forces, the account suggests that the fall of Tyre was only possible with the procurement by Alexander the Great of Phoenician vessels and crews to force simultaneous land and sea engagement.

Phoenician silver didrachm, Tyre mint, c. 332-306 BCE
Bearded Melgarth riding hippocamp, waves and dolphin below
Courtesy of Joseph Sermarini, http://www.forumancientcoins.com

Anger is the one thing made better by delay.

Syrus, Maxims

Case Studies from Hebrew Scripture

Heritage of the Phoenicians

As cited previously, the Phoenicians were descendants of Canaan. The founder of the great Phoenician city of Sidon, mentioned in the first book of the Bible, was Canaan's firstborn son.

> *Canaan was the father of Sidon his firstborn, and of the Hittites, Jebusites, Amorites, Girgashites, Hivites, Arkites, Sinites, Arvadites, Zemarites and Hamathites. Genesis 10:15-18*

Sidon was one of two great Phoenician cites, the other being Tyre. These were predated by Byblos in importance. In the Hebrew scriptures, we shall see quite detailed descriptions of their product line and business partners. The first passage for inspection is that of the prophet Isaiah, as he predicted the fall of Tyre.

Tyre – The Marketplace of Nations

The prophet Isaiah spoke on the forthcoming downfall of Tyre, but in the process, he describes the business dominance of the Phoenician center of trade.

Isaiah 23

A Prophecy About Tyre

1 An oracle concerning Tyre: Wail, O ships of Tarshish! For Tyre is destroyed and left without house or harbor. From the land of Cyprus word has come to them.

2 Be silent, you people of the island and you merchants of Sidon, whom the seafarers have enriched.

3 On the great waters came the grain of the Shihor; the harvest of the Nile was the revenue of Tyre, and she became the marketplace of the nations.

4 Be ashamed, O Sidon, and you, O fortress of the sea, for the sea has spoken: "I have neither been in labor nor given birth; I have neither reared sons nor brought up daughters."

5 When word comes to Egypt, they will be in anguish at the report from Tyre.

6 Cross over to Tarshish; wail, you people of the island.

7 *Is this your city of revelry, the old, old city, whose feet have taken her to settle in far-off lands?*

8 *Who planned this against Tyre, the bestower of crowns, whose merchants are princes, whose traders are renowned in the earth?*

9 *The LORD Almighty planned it, to bring low the pride of all glory and to humble all who are renowned on the earth.*

10 *Till your land as along the Nile, O Daughter of Tarshish, for you no longer have a harbor.*

11 *The LORD has stretched out his hand over the sea and made its kingdoms tremble. He has given an order concerning Phoenicia that her fortresses be destroyed.*

12 *He said, "No more of your reveling, O Virgin Daughter of Sidon, now crushed! "Up, cross over to Cyprus; even there you will find no rest."*

13 *Look at the land of the Babylonians, this people that is now of no account! The Assyrians have made it a place for desert creatures; they raised up their siege towers, they stripped its fortresses bare and turned it into a ruin.*

14 *Wail, you ships of Tarshish; your fortress is destroyed!*

15 *At that time Tyre will be forgotten for seventy years, the span of a king's life. But at the end of these seventy years, it will happen to Tyre as in the song of the prostitute:*

16 *"Take up a harp, walk through the city, O prostitute forgotten; play the harp well, sing many a song, so that you will be remembered."*

17 *At the end of seventy years, the LORD will deal with Tyre. She will return to her hire as a prostitute and will ply her trade with all the kingdoms on the face of the earth.*

18 *Yet her profit and her earnings will be set apart for the LORD; they will not be stored up or hoarded. Her profits will go to those who live before the LORD, for abundant food and fine clothes.*

We see mention of the people of the island in verse 2. This is a reference to the fortress city of Tyre built upon a man-made island. The Sidonians are noted as merchants whom have become rich on the seafaring trade. Verse 3 says that Tyre was indeed the marketplace of the nations. Verse 7 makes a quite profound statement that the Phoenicians have settled far-off lands. As the bestower of crowns in verse 8,

49

Phoenician trade supplied kings and kingdoms, firmly establishing the powers that be. The Phoenicians were referred to by the prophet Isaiah as the best traders on the face of the earth. Unfortunately, pride was to be the downfall of this ancient merchant city. Still, we shall see that kings and wealth may come and go, but the business culture persists in the Phoenician people.

Another Hebrew prophet, Ezekiel, was even more revealing of the Phoenician business empire when reciting a lament concerning the destruction of Tyre.

Ezekiel 27

A Lament for Tyre

1   *The word of the LORD came to me:*

2   *"Son of man, take up a lament concerning Tyre.*

3   *Say to Tyre, situated at the gateway to the sea, merchant of peoples on many coasts, 'This is what the Sovereign LORD says: " 'You say, O Tyre, "I am perfect in beauty."*

4   *Your domain was on the high seas; your builders brought your beauty to perfection.*

5   *They made all your timbers of pine trees from Senir; they took a cedar from Lebanon to make a mast for you.*

6 Of oaks from Bashan they made your oars; of cypress wood from the coasts of Cyprus they made your deck, inlaid with ivory.

7 Fine embroidered linen from Egypt was your sail and served as your banner; your awnings were of blue and purple from the coasts of Elishah.

8 Men of Sidon and Arvad were your oarsmen; your skilled men, O Tyre, were aboard as your seamen.

9 Veteran craftsmen of Gebal were on board as shipwrights to caulk your seams. All the ships of the sea and their sailors came alongside to trade for your wares.

10 " 'Men of Persia, Lydia and Put served as soldiers in your army. They hung their shields and helmets on your walls, bringing you splendor.

11 Men of Arvad and Helech manned your walls on every side; men of Gammad were in your towers. They hung their shields around your walls; they brought your beauty to perfection.

12 " 'Tarshish did business with you because of your great wealth of goods; they exchanged silver, iron, tin and lead for your merchandise.

13 " 'Greece, Tubal and Meshech traded with you; they exchanged slaves and articles of bronze for your wares.

14 " 'Men of Beth Togarmah exchanged work horses, war horses and mules for your merchandise.

15 " 'The men of Rhodes traded with you, and many coastlands were your customers; they paid you with ivory tusks and ebony.

16 " 'Aram did business with you because of your many products; they exchanged turquoise, purple fabric, embroidered work, fine linen, coral and rubies for your merchandise.

17 " 'Judah and Israel traded with you; they exchanged wheat from Minnith and confections, honey, oil and balm for your wares.

18 " 'Damascus, because of your many products and great wealth of goods, did business with you in wine from Helbon and wool from Zahar.

19 " 'Danites and Greeks from Uzal bought your merchandise; they exchanged wrought iron, cassia and calamus for your wares.

20 " 'Dedan traded in saddle blankets with you.

21 " 'Arabia and all the princes of Kedar were your customers; they did business with you in lambs, rams and goats.

22 " 'The merchants of Sheba and Raamah traded with you; for your merchandise they exchanged the finest of all kinds of spices and precious stones, and gold.

23 " 'Haran, Canneh and Eden and merchants of Sheba, Asshur and Kilmad traded with you.

24 In your marketplace they traded with you beautiful garments, blue fabric, embroidered work and multicolored rugs with cords twisted and tightly knotted.

25 " 'The ships of Tarshish serve as carriers for your wares. You are filled with heavy cargo in the heart of the sea.

26 Your oarsmen take you out to the high seas. But the east wind will break you to pieces in the heart of the sea.

27 Your wealth, merchandise and wares, your mariners, seamen and shipwrights, your merchants and all your soldiers, and everyone else on board will sink into the heart of the sea on the day of your shipwreck.

28 The shorelands will quake when your seamen cry out.

29 All who handle the oars will abandon their ships; the mariners and all the seamen will stand on the shore.

30 They will raise their voice and cry bitterly over you; they will sprinkle dust on their heads and roll in ashes.

31 They will shave their heads because of you and will put on sackcloth. They will weep over you with anguish of soul and with bitter mourning.

32 As they wail and mourn over you, they will take up a lament concerning you: "Who was ever silenced like Tyre, surrounded by the sea?"

33 When your merchandise went out on the seas, you satisfied many nations; with your great wealth and your wares you enriched the kings of the earth.

34 Now you are shattered by the sea in the depths of the waters; your wares and all your company have gone down with you.

35 All who live in the coastlands are appalled at you; their kings shudder with horror and their faces are distorted with fear.

36 The merchants among the nations hiss at you; you have come to a horrible end and will be no more.' "

Ezekiel describes Tyre as merchants active on many coasts, a commentary on the expansive trade network setup by the Phoenician businessmen. The lament describes the diverse product line and numerous trading partners. These are recaptured in Table 1. Ezekiel goes on to say, *"When your merchandise went out on the seas, you satisfied many nations; with your great wealth and your wares you enriched the kings of the earth."* The prophet casts a picture of a giant conglomerate, a business machine, unmatched by any on earth, and describes the world-wide sorrow upon the breakup of this trading empire.

A few other items are worth noting in this revealing passage. When looking at this list of considerable size and geographic influence, we see a diverse product line. While cedar made them important local business allies, their business sense called them to become more than just a natural resource supplier – a wholesaler of pre-market goods. The Phoenicians made ships of their resource and generated a marketable service. While they offered seafaring transportation services, the Phoenicians saw opportunity in retail marketing. They essentially cut out the middleman and directly linked product availability to open markets. From Table 1, we also see that the Phoenicians used human resource outsourcing when it made sense. One example cited is in the use of outsourced security forces. In doing this, the Phoenicians leveraged time and resources for business opportunity.

We also see that the people of Tyre, master shipbuilders, used cargo ships of Tarshish. The ships of Tarshish were large payload vessels of advanced design. The location of Tarshish was secondary to the fact that the Phoenicians developed and implemented the shipping technology required to support their trade capacity and grow their business.

Phoenician bronze coin, Simyra mint, c. 2nd century BCE
Obverse: Diademed head of Zeus
Reverse: Turrented bust of Tyche within wreath
Courtesy of Joseph Sermarini, http://www.forumancientcoins.com

TraDEAbLes™

Table 1. Partial list of goods and services of the Phoenicians and their trading partners, as cited by the prophet Ezekiel.

Business Partner	Goods or Services Secured	Comments
Senir	Pine	
Lebanon	Cedar	Internal natural resources
Bashan	Oak	
Cyprus	Cyprus	
Egypt	embroidered linen	
Elishah	blue & purple dye	
Sidon and Arvad	Oarsmen	Human resource
Tyre	Seamen	Human resource
Craftsmen of Gebal	ship maintenance	
Persia, Lydia and Put	Mercenaries	Outsourcing
Arvad, Helech, & Gammad	Security	Outsourcing
Tarshish	silver, iron, tin, lead	
Greece, Tubal & Meshech	slaves, bronze	
Beth Togarmah	work horses, war horses, mules	
Rhodes	ivory, ebony	
Aram	turquoise, purple fabric, embroidered work, fine linen, coral and rubies	
Judah and Israel	wheat, honey, oil, balm	
Damascus	wine, wool	
Danites and Greeks	wrought iron, cassia and calamus	
Dedan	saddle blankets	
Arabia	lambs, rams, goats	
Sheba and Raamah	spices, precious stones, gold	
Haran, Canneh, Eden, Sheba, Asshur and Kilmad	garments, blue fabric, embroidered work and multicolored rugs	

Ancient Negotiating Scripts

Payment to Hiram: von Christoph Weigel, Biblia ectypa. Bildnussen auss Heilige Schrifft dess Alt- und Neuen Testaments. Augsburg, Germany, 1787.

King David and King Hiram

While we have gleaned the extensive product line and expansive trade latitude of the Phoenicians from Hebrew prophets, nowhere do we get better insight into the makings of a deal than in the exchanges

TraDEAbLes™

documented in the Bible concerning the biggest business proposition of ancient times – the most extravagant building project on record, the construction of the Hebrew temple to house the Ark of the Covenant, the place where God's presence dwelt. This deal led to an even deeper business alliance and ushered Tyre towards the pinnacle of its business empire, for King Solomon was the wisest and riches man throughout history. The Phoenicians brought the world's wealth to Solomon. Let us examine the business dealings of the Phoenician King Hiram of Tyre in detail which are well documented in multiple locations within the Hebrew Scriptures.

King David, the same David who slew the giant Goliath as a youth, became the second king over Israel. It was not without immense friction, as King Saul was jealous of David and attempted to spear him in his own palace on more than one occasion while David strummed a harp. Saul was tormented in spirit, for out of disobedience, he was told that God would replace him as king. Music was his only solace. Saul offered his daughter in marriage to David, hoping that the dowry would cost him his life, for acquiring it involved killing 100 Philistines. David killed 200. David was forced to flee for his life, but Saul, with army in tow, pursued him. An even greater twist was that Saul's son Jonathan, the heir to the throne, and David were best of friends. When Saul and Jonathan were killed in battle on the same day, David became king over all Israel, though he was anointed so by the prophet Samuel nearly two decades earlier, while just a boy. All this did not escape the watchful eye of King Hiram, who quietly avoided the extensive regional conflict, especially fierce between the Philistines and Israelites.

Once David had been installed on the throne, King Hiram sent an envoy bearing extensive gifts – Tradeables™. 1 Chronicles 14:1 says, *"Now Hiram king of Tyre sent messengers to David, along with cedar logs, stonemasons and carpenters to build a palace for him."* This was neither part of a business deal nor a request of the region's newest monarch, but King Hiram took a proactive approach to lay the foundation for a long-term business alliance. Hiram offered choice cedar and skilled laborers – a gift that was not refused and made a lasting impression. This was no doubt a costly gesture, but Hiram had made a wise investment. His gift diffused any notion of political challenge and affirmed Hiram's belief that this kingdom was the new seat of regional power. A new king would, of course, require much more than a few pieces of wood, and Hiram wielded the trade network which could satisfy those needs. King David had two means to acquire goods: buy them or seize the plunder of conquered nations. He did both. David rode with the army, while Hiram brought the best the world had to offer to David's doorstep – a wonderful business relationship.

The palace was indeed built, and sometime later, David became uneasy. As told in 2 Samuel 7, he said to Nathan the prophet, *"Here I am, living in a palace of cedar, while the ark of God remains in a tent."* Initially, Nathan's word to David was to do whatever God put on his heart, but that night, God gave another message for David. Since David was a warrior and had shed much blood, he was not to be the one to build the temple. It was to be his successor, Solomon, who would build the temple of God as a man of peace. In turn for his desire to build a dwelling far superior to his own for the ark, God said he would establish David's house as an eternal kingdom, preserving the earthly line of David's successors. Still, the builder would be in need of plans and a bounty of supplies, so David amassed huge quantities of raw materials awaiting the proper time for construction.

When the time had come for Solomon to reign, David charged his son with the responsibilities of the kingdom and the task of building the temple.

1 Chronicles 28

> *10 Consider now, for the LORD has chosen you to build a temple as a sanctuary. Be strong and do the work."*
>
> *11 Then David gave his son Solomon the plans for the portico of the temple, its buildings, its storerooms, its upper parts, its inner rooms and the place of atonement.*
>
> *12 He gave him the plans of all that the Spirit had put in his mind for the courts of the temple of the LORD and all the surrounding rooms, for the treasuries of the temple of God and for the treasuries for the dedicated things.*

13 *He gave him instructions for the divisions of the priests and Levites, and for all the work of serving in the temple of the LORD, as well as for all the articles to be used in its service.*

14 *He designated the weight of gold for all the gold articles to be used in various kinds of service, and the weight of silver for all the silver articles to be used in various kinds of service:*

15 *the weight of gold for the gold lampstands and their lamps, with the weight for each lampstand and its lamps; and the weight of silver for each silver lampstand and its lamps, according to the use of each lampstand;*

16 *the weight of gold for each table for consecrated bread; the weight of silver for the silver tables;*

17 *the weight of pure gold for the forks, sprinkling bowls and pitchers; the weight of gold for each gold dish; the weight of silver for each silver dish;*

18 *and the weight of the refined gold for the altar of incense. He also gave him the plan for the chariot, that is, the cherubim of gold that spread their wings and shelter the ark of the covenant of the LORD.*

TraDEAbLes™

> 19 "All this," David said, "I have in writing from the hand of the LORD upon me, and he gave me understanding in all the details of the plan."
>
> 20 David also said to Solomon his son, "Be strong and courageous, and do the work. Do not be afraid or discouraged, for the LORD God, my God, is with you. He will not fail you or forsake you until all the work for the service of the temple of the LORD is finished. 21 The divisions of the priests and Levites are ready for all the work on the temple of God, and every willing man skilled in any craft will help you in all the work. The officials and all the people will obey your every command."

We see that extensive preparations were made, and Solomon simply needed to get started. In the next chapter, we see the enormity of these provisions. David had specified the quantity of gold or silver going into each utensil, and we see in the next passage that this sum was provided and more.

1 Chronicles 29

> 1 Then King David said to the whole assembly: "My son Solomon, the one whom God has chosen, is young and inexperienced. The task is great, because this palatial structure is not for man but for the LORD God.

> 2 *With all my resources I have provided for the temple of my God—gold for the gold work, silver for the silver, bronze for the bronze, iron for the iron and wood for the wood, as well as onyx for the settings, turquoise, stones of various colors, and all kinds of fine stone and marble—all of these in large quantities.*
>
> 3 *Besides, in my devotion to the temple of my God I now give my personal treasures of gold and silver for the temple of my God, over and above everything I have provided for this holy temple:*
>
> 4 *three thousand talents of gold (gold of Ophir) and seven thousand talents of refined silver, for the overlaying of the walls of the buildings,*
>
> 5 *for the gold work and the silver work, and for all the work to be done by the craftsmen. Now, who is willing to consecrate himself today to the LORD?"*

The people answered this challenge with even more gifts.

> 1 Chronicles 29
>
> 6 *Then the leaders of families, the officers of the tribes of Israel, the commanders of thousands and commanders of hundreds,*

TraDEAbLes™

and the officials in charge of the king's work gave willingly.

7 *They gave toward the work on the temple of God five thousand talents and ten thousand darics of gold, ten thousand talents of silver, eighteen thousand talents of bronze and a hundred thousand talents* [h] *of iron.*

8 *Any who had precious stones gave them to the treasury of the temple of the LORD in the custody of Jehiel the Gershonite.*

9 *The people rejoiced at the willing response of their leaders, for they had given freely and wholeheartedly to the LORD. David the king also rejoiced greatly.*

To have an appreciation for the size of these gifts, the amounts of each material cited are given in Table 2 in today's units. Note that these were personal donations that were added to sums set aside from the royal treasury. Yet, even more material would be necessary, and the monumental task of construction and adornment remained.

Table 2. Gifts in today's equivalent units for building the temple of God in addition to designated amounts from the royal treasury.

Raw Material	David's Gift *Tons*	People's Gift *Tons*
Gold	110	190
Silver	260	375
Bronze	-	675
Iron	-	3,750

Julius Schnorr von Carolsfeld, c. 1851-60
Solomon Builds the Temple

TraDEAbLes™

King Solomon and King Hiram

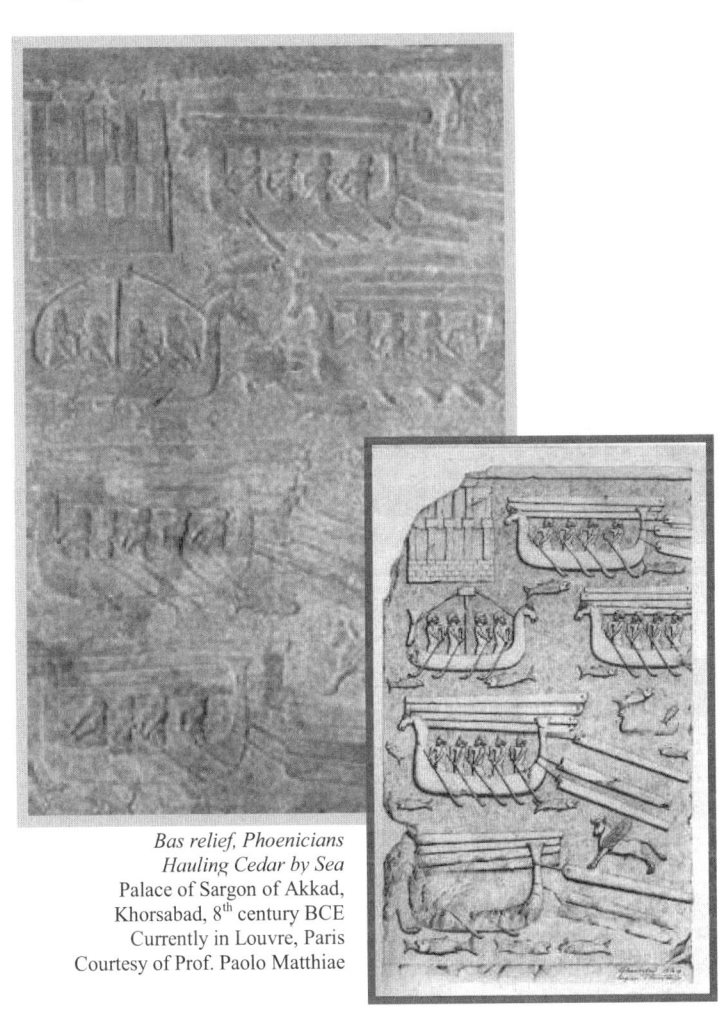

*Bas relief, Phoenicians
Hauling Cedar by Sea*
Palace of Sargon of Akkad,
Khorsabad, 8th century BCE
Currently in Louvre, Paris
Courtesy of Prof. Paolo Matthiae

Artist's rendering upon discovery, 1844
Eugene Flandin, Chief Artist,
Excavations of Paul-Emile Botta
after Albenda, 1986

Upon his father's death, Solomon sacrificed to his god, who appeared to him in a dream. When asked what he desired, Solomon replied, *"... give your servant a discerning heart to govern your people and to distinguish between right and wrong."* Solomon could have asked for long life, wealth, and power, but he requested wisdom. By choosing wisely, God also gave him all the things he did not request. The Bible says, *"Men of all nations came to listen to Solomon's wisdom, sent by all the kings of the world, who had heard of his wisdom."* Solomon is designated as the wisest man to have ever lived. A wise man would surely also be so in business dealings.

In Chapter 5 of 1 Kings, we have a rich exchange between Solomon and King Hiram and the motherload of all business deals. King Hiram was also quick to continue the relationship with the son as he had with the father. 1 Kings 5:1 says, *"When Hiram king of Tyre heard that Solomon had been anointed king to succeed his father David, he sent his envoys to Solomon, because he had always been on friendly terms with David."* Solomon sent back this reply.

1 Kings 5

3 *"You know that because of the wars waged against my father David from all sides, he could not build a temple for the Name of the LORD his God until the LORD put his enemies under his feet.*

TraDEAbLes™

> *4 But now the LORD my God has given me rest on every side, and there is no adversary or disaster.*
>
> *5 I intend, therefore, to build a temple for the Name of the LORD my God, as the LORD told my father David, when he said, 'Your son whom I will put on the throne in your place will build the temple for my Name.'*
>
> *6 So give orders that cedars of Lebanon be cut for me. My men will work with yours, and I will pay you for your men whatever wages you set. You know that we have no one so skilled in felling timber as the Sidonians."*

Solomon spoke openly with Hiram of his divine mission. In doing so, he implied the need for quality materials and workmanship. He also offered to labor jointly in this effort, for who better for his own workers to learn from than the best. Solomon says they have no one so skilled, paying the Phoenician people the highest of compliments. But ... did you catch the terms of the deal? No, the price was not negotiated. This was a carte blanche offer – a BLANK CHECK! Would the wisest and richest man in the world not care about price? Surely, he did, yet he already held fast to that level of trust earned from past relationship. Would Hiram exploit this opportunity to run up the price? No, Hiram was interested in the long-term relationship. They both would prosper together.

1 Kings 5

7 *When Hiram heard Solomon's message, he was greatly pleased and said, "Praise be to the LORD today, for he has given David a wise son to rule over this great nation."*

8 *So Hiram sent word to Solomon: "I have received the message you sent me and will do all you want in providing the cedar and pine logs.*

9 *My men will haul them down from Lebanon to the sea, and I will float them in rafts by sea to the place you specify. There I will separate them and you can take them away. And you are to grant my wish by providing food for my royal household."*

10 *In this way Hiram kept Solomon supplied with all the cedar and pine logs he wanted,*

11 *and Solomon gave Hiram twenty thousand cors of wheat as food for his household, in addition to twenty thousand baths of pressed olive oil. Solomon continued to do this for Hiram year after year.*

12 *The LORD gave Solomon wisdom, just as he had promised him. There were peaceful relations between Hiram and Solomon, and the two of them made a treaty.*

TraDEAbLes™

13 King Solomon conscripted laborers from all Israel—thirty thousand men.

14 He sent them off to Lebanon in shifts of ten thousand a month, so that they spent one month in Lebanon and two months at home. Adoniram was in charge of the forced labor.

15 Solomon had seventy thousand carriers and eighty thousand stonecutters in the hills,

16 as well as thirty-three hundred foremen who supervised the project and directed the workmen.

17 At the king's command they removed from the quarry large blocks of quality stone to provide a foundation of dressed stone for the temple.

18 The craftsmen of Solomon and Hiram and the men of Gebal cut and prepared the timber and stone for the building of the temple.

So how did King Hiram handle his blank check? Wait a minute! Did Hiram specify the terms? He simply asked Solomon to provide food for his household. So how much was that? Another open ended deal! We are later given quantities that Solomon actually sent as annual payment. It must have been enough. Take caution before you extend too many blank checks! Such a business deal was cultivated long before this conversation. Recall the use of Tradeables™ first introduced in this business relationship when there was no deal (or the eventual dealer) on the scene. That opened the door, but King Hiram, no doubt, supplied the royal family and household with plenty of goods in the intervening years. The Phoenicians dealt shrewdly with clients and delivered quality. This led to the avenue of trust seen between these two parties in this deal.

So, the workers got to work on this massive construction project. In scale, it was not an impressive structure, but the materials and detail made it the top construction project of all time. The interior was to be paneled in cedar fully carved in ornamental flowers. The inner sanctuary was of cedar overlaid with pure gold. Its pillars were to be of cast bronze. Cherubim of olive wood covered with gold were to span the inner sanctuary. The artisanship had to be the best, so Solomon turned once again to King Hiram. From a different account of the same transaction between Solomon and King Hiram, we find a few additional elements.

2 Chronicles 2

3   *Solomon sent this message to Hiram king of Tyre:*
    "Send me cedar logs as you did for my father David when you sent him cedar to build a palace to live in.

4 Now I am about to build a temple for the Name of the LORD my God and to dedicate it to him for burning fragrant incense before him, for setting out the consecrated bread regularly, and for making burnt offerings every morning and evening and on Sabbaths and New Moons and at the appointed feasts of the LORD our God. This is a lasting ordinance for Israel.

5 "The temple I am going to build will be great, because our God is greater than all other gods.

6 But who is able to build a temple for him, since the heavens, even the highest heavens, cannot contain him? Who then am I to build a temple for him, except as a place to burn sacrifices before him?

7 "Send me, therefore, a man skilled to work in gold and silver, bronze and iron, and in purple, crimson and blue yarn, and experienced in the art of engraving, to work in Judah and Jerusalem with my skilled craftsmen, whom my father David provided.

8 "Send me also cedar, pine and algum logs from Lebanon, for I know that your men are skilled in cutting timber there. My men will work with yours

> 9 to provide me with plenty of lumber, because the temple I build must be large and magnificent.
>
> 10 I will give your servants, the woodsmen who cut the timber, twenty thousand cors of ground wheat, twenty thousand cors of barley, twenty thousand baths of wine and twenty thousand baths of olive oil."

First, we find mention of a past business deal and a desire to continue this business relationship on behalf of Solomon. Next, we see reference to the skill level required in the project, not just in the felling of trees, as seen in the prior passage. Surely artisans existed amongst the Israelites, but apparently none were so skilled in working with metals and embroidered linen as found in the Phoenician society. Solomon requests assignment of a Phoenician artisan to perform the most complicated and extravagant tasks in finishing out the temple. This account is more detailed and perhaps is a follow-on conversation to that recorded in I Kings. It reads more as a summary or a call to action on that which had already been discussed. Here, Solomon even gives the settled on terms of wheat, barley, wine, and olive oil.

The reply also contains detail on the add-on request. Hiram was to send Huram-Abi, a man of mixed Phoenician-Jewish heritage – a man of great skill. Notice how the exchange of compliments precedes business, laying the groundwork for openness. Still, there is much more to be extracted from Hiram's

TraDEAbLes™

response – clues as to why a Hebrew king could have such a strong working relationship with a man of Canaanite descent.

> *11 Hiram king of Tyre replied by letter to Solomon:*
> *"Because the LORD loves his people, he has made you their king."*
>
> *12 And Hiram added: "Praise be to the LORD, the God of Israel, who made heaven and earth! He has given King David a wise son, endowed with intelligence and discernment, who will build a temple for the LORD and a palace for himself.*
>
> *13 I am sending you Huram-Abi, a man of great skill,*
>
> *14 whose mother was from Dan and whose father was from Tyre. He is trained to work in gold and silver, bronze and iron, stone and wood, and with purple and blue and crimson yarn and fine linen. He is experienced in all kinds of engraving and can execute any design given to him. He will work with your craftsmen and with those of my Lord, David your father.*
>
> *15 Now let my Lord send his servants the wheat and barley and the olive oil and wine he promised,*

> *16 and we will cut all the logs from Lebanon that you need and will float them in rafts by sea down to Joppa. You can then take them up to Jerusalem."*
>
> *17 Solomon took a census of all the aliens who were in Israel, after the census his father David had taken; and they were found to be 153,600.*
>
> *18 He assigned 70,000 of them to be carriers and 80,000 to be stonecutters in the hills, with 3,600 foremen over them to keep the people working.*

Wow! Here we get the specifics – the when, where, and how. The cedar was to be floated to Joppa and hauled to Jerusalem. Don't overlook the manpower assigned to this task – 153,600 non-Hebrew residents conscripted into service.

Take a look back at verse 12. King Hiram uses for the second time the name for God, LORD, which the New International Version of the Bible transcribes in place of Yahweh. He said, *"Praise be to the LORD, the God of Israel, who made the heaven and earth!"* Now, the Phoenicians may not have allowed religion to be a stumbling block to business dealings, but to invoke the most holy name of God, giving him praise, and acknowledging him as the creator goes beyond business politeness. On this note, Johnston (1965) commented,

TraDEAbLes™

The overtures of Hiram to Solomon could not fail, therefore, to have been viewed with grave suspicion by the priesthood, if the affection existing between the Tyrian and the Jewish monarchs had not had its root in a religious sympathy of a wholly different character from that which could have been possible at any later date, for between the pure and exalted worship of Jehovah and that of Baal there was a whole world of difference (p.116).

Was King Hiram a worshipper of the God of the Israelites? Had he renounced the Baal worship prevalent in his culture? We may never know for sure, but it is doubtful that King Hiram would have put on a ruse just to swing a business deal. His sincerity appears genuine. His actions endorse his authenticity.

Now, was Huram-Abi a Tradeable™? He was not part of the original deal. Must Tradeables™ be unsolicited, for Solomon surely makes the request? Was the deal in jeopardy if the added artisan was not supplied? Probably not, but it was in Hiram's best interest to send the best, not only to perform the task to satisfaction, but to oversee the quality of the project. Did Solomon request Huram-Abi? No, the choice was left to King Hiram, so the selection of Huram-Abi may have indeed been a Tradeable™. Solomon asked for a skilled craftsman; Hiram chose to send the best – a most likely Tradeable™. In 1 Kings 7:13, we find where Solomon sent for Huram, but no doubt, this was another call to action after the selection was finalized.

Huram-Abi's work was exceptional and certainly gained leverage for future deals. Yet, the business relationship was so mature at this stage, was there need for further leverage? If the business relationship continues, there is always need for increased leverage. Other building projects followed, all requiring materials to be supplied by King Hiram, including a second palace known as the Hall of the Forest of Lebanon and a separate palace for Solomon's Egyptian wife. Each project was more demanding from a materials perspective than the last.

Following the twenty-year building project collaboration on the temple and king's palace, King Solomon sent an unsolicited gift to King Hiram to show his pleasure – twenty cities in the region around Galilee. When Hiram went to inspect his gift, he was less than pleased. He questioned Solomon, *"What kind of towns are these you have given me, my brother?"* Even when delivering a negative report, King Hiram directs the focus of criticism onto the gift and away from the relationship by calling him "my brother" in the same sentence. We are not given any follow-up on the disposition of these towns, but Solomon's use of Tradeables™ was not very effective in this instance. Effective use of Tradeables™ involves meeting a client's need unrelated to the business deal. These towns apparently did not meet a need – a lesson to all wishing to practice Tradeables™ for more robust negotiations.

TraDEAbLes™

Hiram Shows the Plans to Solomon, J. J. Scheuchzer. Physica Sacra Iconibus Illustrata, Augsburg, 1731.

Depiction of the bronze sea cast by Huram-Abi, Unknown illustrator. L'Histoire du Vieux et du Nouveau Testament, Nicolás Fontaine, 1670

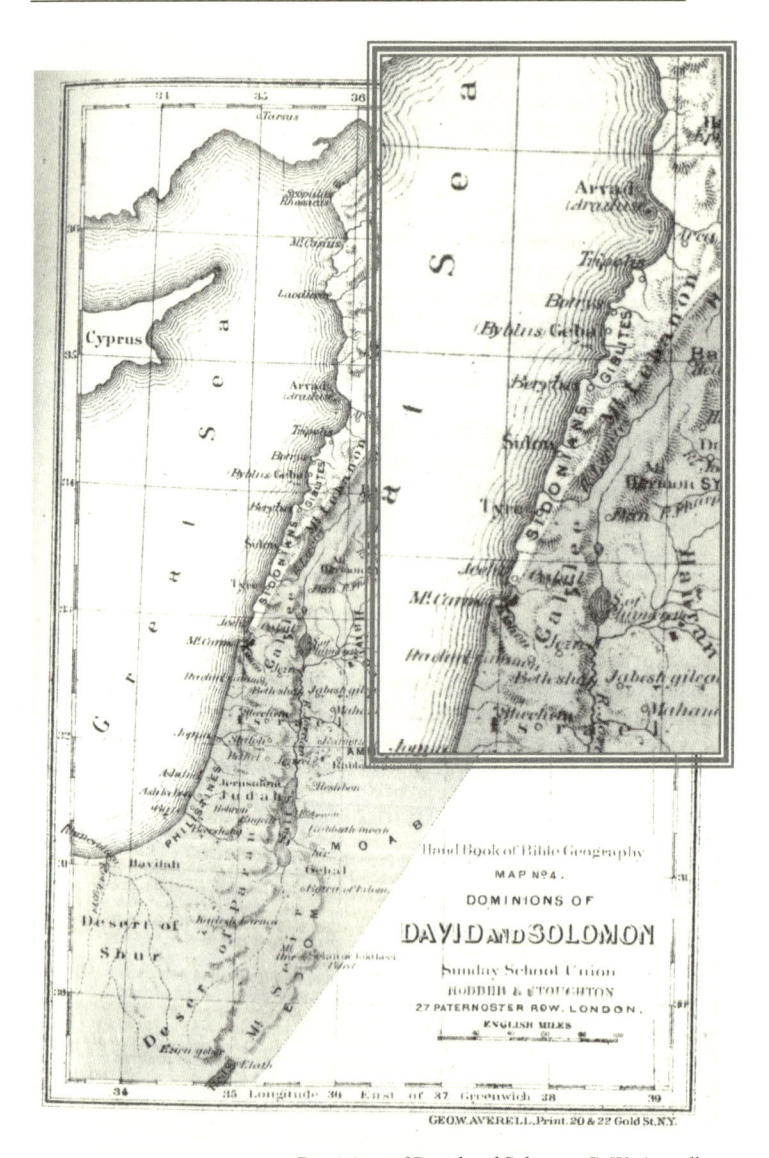

Dominions of David and Solomon, G. W. Averell
Hand Book of Bible Geography, Map No.4
Hodder & Stroughton, London, 1870
Kings David and Solomon preserved the sovereignty of Phoenicia proper

TraDEAbLes™

Commentary Outside the Scriptures

The account of the letter exchange given to us in the historical record of Josephus is nearly identical to that in the Hebrew scriptures, so it need not be duplicated. However, Josephus adds (Jewish Antiquities, VIII.2.8.58), "*So the friendship between Hiram and Solomon hereby increased more and more; and they swore to continue it forever.*" Josephus also records (VIII.2.8) a further exchange of wit which characterized the intimacy of the relationship.

> *(109) and in their annals the building of our temple is related; for Hiram, the king of Tyre, was the friend of Solomon our king, and had such friendship transmitted down to him from his forefathers.*

> *(110) He thereupon was ambitious to contribute to the splendor of this edifice of Solomon, and made him a present of one hundred and twenty talents of gold. He also cut down the most excellent timber out of that mountain which is called Libanus, and sent it to him for adorning its roof. Solomon also not only made him many other presents, by way of requital, but gave him a country in Galilee also, that was called Cabul.*

> *(111) But there was another passion, a philosophic inclination of theirs, which cemented the friendship that was between them; for they sent mutual problems to one another, with a*

desire to have them unriddled by each other; wherein Solomon was superior to Hiram, as he was wiser than he in other respects; and many of the letters that passed between them are still preserved among the Tyrians.

Josephus quotes that Dius, author of the *History of the Phoenicians*, independently wrote of this riddle exchange, but adds that a great deal of money was at stake in the process. According to Dius, Hiram owed a great sum until he found a man of Tyre named Abdemon who was able to solve Solomon's riddles and pose additional ones in exchange. Some suggest that the gift of cities to Hiram was, in fact, a payment for this friendly wagering.

There is mention of one more solidifying gift between the kings. According to Eusebius (praep. Evan. X. 99), *"a marriage was contracted between Solomon and a daughter of Hiram as the most satisfactory way of cementing the union* (p. 121)." In I Kings 11:1, it says, *"King Solomon, however, loved many foreign women besides Pharaoh's daughter – Moabites, Ammonites, Edomites, Sidonians, and Hittites."* With the specific citation of Sidonians and the mention of seven hundred wives of royal birth in following verses, the accuracy of this statement is corroborated in spirit. Thus, there was a familial bond between the houses of Hiram and Solomon, though the strength of that attachment may have been diluted by the shear number of rival wives.

Rebuilding the Temple

Kings came and went. Wisdom did as well. Solomon's son did not exercise wisdom and had all but Judah striped from him as a result. The Israelites were told that a loss of faith would result in exile. Following the reign of King Hezekiah, the Babylonians invaded Jerusalem, destroying the temple, carrying off its treasures, and taking captives those who survived.

It is from Babylon that we get the famous stories of Shadrach, Meshach, and Abdenego's trial by fire and Daniel's visit to the lion's den. After the prophesied 70 years of captivity, those wishing to return to Jerusalem were allowed to do so. The Persian kings that displaced the Babylonian rulers even paid for the reconstruction of the wall and the temple. Articles of gold, silver, and bronze used in the temple service were returned.

Another building project required replacement timber. With the remnant allowed to return from captivity by Cyrus, king of Persia, the business relationship with the tenders of the forests of Lebanon continued. In Ezra 3:7, we are told, "*Then they gave money to the masons and carpenters, and gave food and drink and oil to the people of Sidon and Tyre, so that they would bring cedar logs by sea from Lebanon to Joppa, as authorized by Cyrus king of Persia.*" The same methods, route, and form of payment used to supply the building of the original temple were used to recapture some of the temple's former glory in its rebuilding. Craftsmanship and product never left the Phoenician's repertoire.

A Counter Example

When we speak in generalities on best practices of the Phoenicians, we certainly do not infer that these qualities were enjoyed by all. A noted counterexample is that of Jezebel, daughter of Ittobaal, who became king of Tyre in 887 BCE. Jezebel was given in marriage to Ahab, king of Israel. Jezebel was religiously intolerant and instituted Baal worship as the national religion, executing the 'prophets of the LORD'. Her character and exploits are well documented in the book of 1 Kings in the biblical account of the prophet Elijah.

When we cite qualities and traits of the Phoenicians, we emphasize those elements which led to greatness. We highlight those qualities worth emulating for better business deals and business relationships, recognizing and discounting atypical characters and characteristics.

When you have just climbed out of a deep well and are perched on top, you are in the greatest danger of falling again.

Plautus, Miles Gloriosus

TraDEAbLes™

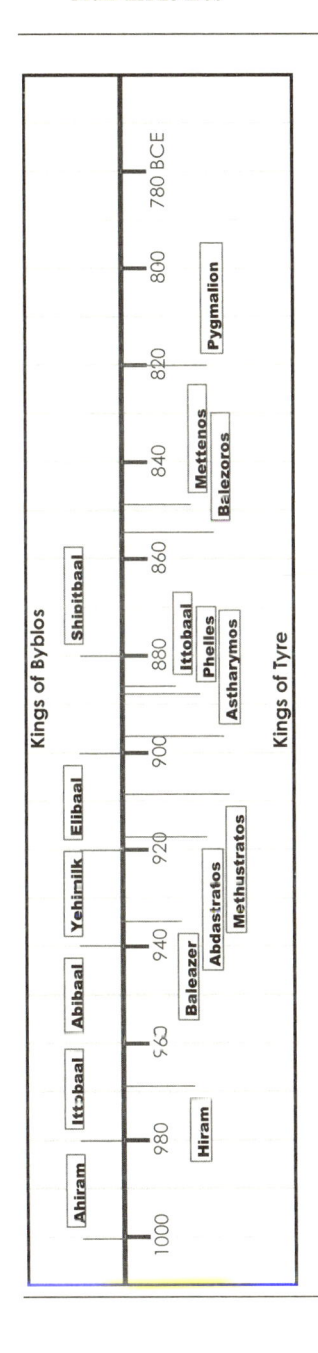

Chronology of the Phoenician kings in Byblos and Tyre from 1000 BCE through Pygmalion, whose exiled daughter founded Carthage as a Phoenician colony on the African coast (as given by Moscati, 1968).

Case Studies from Christian Scripture

Some 2000 years after the business dealings of Solomon and King Hiram, the Phoenician political empire was dismantled. The trade routes were overrun by others, and the cities of Tyre and Sidon were a whisper of what they used to be. The prophecies of Isaiah and Ezekiel had come to pass. One would think that the Phoenician culture had disappeared and the business sense lost forever. However, we see glimpses of the same business savvy in selected Christian scriptures.

The Faith of a Syrophoenician Woman

Jesus and the woman of Canaan, MERIAN, Matthaeus the Elder, 1625. Engraving in *Icones Biblicae*.

TraDEAbLes™

In the Gospels of Matthew and Mark, we have a dual-accounting of a conversation between Jesus and a woman from Sidon, a Phoenician woman. One might presume that the business savvy that brought the Phoenicians to the position of trade preeminence rested in the businessmen. However, here we see the practice of many of those same principles by a Phoenician woman.

Jesus had been teaching, preaching, and healing around the Sea of Galilee. Large crowds were following him everywhere he went. He had just performed the miracle of feeding 5000 men on two fish and five loaves of bread. His disciples had just witnessed him walking on the water. Mark 6:56 says, *"And wherever he went – into villages, towns, or countryside – they placed the sick in the marketplaces. They begged him to let them touch even the edge of his cloak, and all who touched him were healed."* Such was the stage for an unusual encounter.

Mark 7

24 Jesus left that place and went to the vicinity of Tyre. He entered a house and did not want anyone to know it; yet he could not keep his presence secret.

25 In fact, as soon as she heard about him, a woman whose little daughter was possessed by an evil spirit came and fell at his feet.

26 The woman was a Greek, born in Syrian Phoenicia. She begged Jesus to drive the demon out of her daughter.

27 "First let the children eat all they want," he told her, "for it is not right to take the children's bread and toss it to their dogs."

28 "Yes, Lord," she replied, "but even the dogs under the table eat the children's crumbs."

29 Then he told her, "For such a reply, you may go; the demon has left your daughter."

30 She went home and found her child lying on the bed, and the demon gone.

While this does not look much like a business deal, it was a real life negotiation in which a Phoenician woman displayed her faith, persistence, and communication skills. Her daughter was demon-possessed. She approached Jesus with faith that he could heal her daughter. First of all, Jews and Gentiles of that day did not socialize. They avoided one another. It was also not customary for a man and woman to speak in public, even if they were man and wife. Thus, it was unusual that this conversation even took place.

The dialogue was quite terse, as Jesus was at first unwilling to help her, since she was not Jewish. He initially ignored her. "*I was sent only to the lost sheep of Israel*," he told her in the account in the Gospel of

Matthew. Still, she continued to cry out for help. Jesus replied, "*It is not right to take the children's bread and toss it to their dogs.*" She, however, showed her wisdom and, perhaps, her culture's keen business sense in her reply. She said, "*Yes, Lord, but even the dogs eat the crumbs that fall from their masters' table.*" Then Jesus answered, "*Woman, you have great faith! Your request is granted.*" She received the healing requested.

This woman may well have rejected the Baal worship of her ancestry. She professed her faith in Jesus as Lord, knowing that he was her only hope. Despite persistent rebuff by the disciples and by Jesus, she persisted until she received her desired outcome. One expects words of wisdom to come from Jesus, but in this case, she responded wisely with incredible courage and conviction. The Phoenician woman knew what she wanted, she knew where to get it, she was persistent, and she used persuasive words to achieve her goal, despite great odds. She cut across political and social barriers to close the matter to the satisfaction of all.

Ending a Quarrel

There is a very brief encounter recorded in the Christians scriptures involving the people of Tyre and Sidon following the life and ministry of Jesus Christ. While short, it is no less insightful into the mindset of the Phoenician remnant.

Acts 12

19b Then Herod went from Judea to Caesarea and stayed there a while.

20 He had been quarreling with the people of Tyre and Sidon; they now joined together and sought an audience with him. Having secured the support of Blastus, a trusted personal servant of the king, they asked for peace, because they depended on the king's country for their food supply.

An unknown problem arose between the Roman-installed Jewish ruler and the people of Tyre and Sidon. First, it is interesting that a king would have a persisting quarrel with his subjects. Herod Antipas was not one to tolerate disobedience. John the Baptist lost his head because of his finger of accusation pointing towards the throne (Matthew 14:3-12). Herod had married his half-brother's wife, which was commonplace in that time after the death of a sibling. However, Philip was alive and well. This, however, was not the same Herod that probed the Magi concerning the birth of the Messiah. This was Herod the Great's youngest surviving son. In order to protect his monarchy, Herod the Great had two older sons, Alexander and Aristobulus, executed in 7 BCE (Hoehner, 1980). Three other sons were passed over as heirs for mistrust. It was, however, the people of Tyre and Sidon who approached the ruling son to end a quarrel.

TraDEAbLes™

Foremost, we see that the people joined together. There is power in unity. It was to everyone's benefit to keep the peace. Second, they not only joined together, but they sought an audience with the king. They knew the level at which this problem could be solved. However, they did not go in unprepared and on their own. The Phoenicians knew the decision-maker (the king) and a key decision-influencer. They enlisted the support of a trusted personal servant to the king. Their request was for peace. Why? These people knew that this quarrel was not worth the price, for they depended upon the king for their food supply. The people of Tyre and Sidon banded together with a plan and a purpose. They evaluated the consequence of a failure to reconcile and decided the risk was too great. We see in this short description a business savvy reminiscent of prior generations.

For it is in giving that we receive.

St. Francis of Assisi

Summary of Phoenician Negotiating Principles

Here's a summary of biblical principles of Phoenician business success:

- Know your product
- Know your customer
- Know your competition
- Know key business decision-makers
- Foster relations with decision-influencers
- Turn a competitor into a business ally
- Find your niche
- Deliver a quality product
- Diversify
- Expand markets
- Develop a network
- Earn trust
- Choose your words carefully
- Keep focus on your desired outcome
- Remember your limits
- Stay united
- Keep the peace
- Diffuse tension
- Cut out the middleman
- Honor customer loyalty
- Remain humble
- Wrap bad news in a Twinkie
- Be there for the long term
- USE TRADEABLES™!

TraDEAbLes™

Phoenicians bearing gifts (detail), Persepolis relief, 5th century BCE
Courtesy of the Oriental Institute, University of Chicago
Copyright © 1998

Fortune favours the brave.

Terence, Phormi

Chapter III. Modern Negotiations and Use of Tradeables™

3D software rendering of an ancient galley
Courtesy of Peter Solodov

The use of Tradeables™ was not invented by the Phoenicians, though they were especially resourceful in their use. We can benefit from their example to leverage deals in our modern times. Filling a customer need is not an ancient concept. Let's explore more contemporary use of Tradeables™ through a series of case studies, but first, we want to define an element, common in most negotiations, *moments of tension*. Overcoming moments of tension can lead us naturally towards closing the DEAL. Failure to handle moments of tension properly can drive our partner away from the negotiating table. Tradeables™ can even assist us through these perilous times.

Moments of Tension

We define moments of tension when two or more people are going through a tense situation, such as a negotiation between an employee and employer for a raise of salary. The moment the employee requests the raise increase, a moment of tension between the parties is created. We have noticed that there are cultures that create more moments of tension than others. These moments of tension could appear anywhere in the sales cycle or the purchasing process, from prospecting to negotiating the contract. It is more frequent at contract negotiating; however, there are cultures that create moments of tension even upon the customer's first sales visit. Clearly, the Phoenicians approaching King Herod were experiencing a calculated moment of tension.

Understanding that moments of tension exist, it is important, foremost, to recognize them so that we can come equipped with strategies to minimize the tension. When immersed in the situation, it is difficult to remain objective and subdue a natural emotional response unless we have a coping strategy. We have found that preparation before the negotiation, in addition to identifying Tradeables™, helps minimize these moments of tension. Again falling back on the same historical example, the Phoenicians approached the king with a prepared position and a strategy.

When parties enter a negotiation, they do so from either a cooperative or competitive stance. These behaviors permeate all phases of the negotiation. Moments of tension arise as soon as one party enters a competitive mode. This classically comes when negotiating price, but tension can be created at any point in the process. The horizontal axis on Figure III.1.a represents the purchasing process and its various phases: identify needs, search for solutions, search for internal or external suppliers, request for proposals, proposal analysis, proposal selection, negotiation, execution, and new needs. The vertical axis spans the range from cooperative to competitive behavior of the negotiating parties. Figure III.1.a shows an instance where a moment of tension is created in the negotiation phase. This is created between the buyer and seller because of an asymmetry in the negotiation. In this case, one party is willing to cooperate, but the other just wants to get the best outcome for himself.

An asymmetry could also be generated if one party is prepared, and the other isn't. The prepared side could guide cooperatively the other side to a DEAL by using Tradeables™, thus minimizing moments of tension. On the other hand, the prepared party could take advantage of the other side's lack of preparation to make a better

DEAL for himself. If this aggressive behavior is sensed, a moment of tension will be created. The ill-prepared, however, could leave the table thinking he made a great DEAL, only to find out later that he was outmaneuvered. This leads to anguish for the other side. We believe this is a common cause for failure to honor contracts, which spawns legal action. Figure III.1.b shows how moments of tension can come at any point in the purchasing cycle, even at the beginning. A simple example might be showing up late for an appointment. This could pass a cultural norm, but it could also generate high anxiety.

To minimize this and similar moments of tension, the negotiating parties need to search for Tradeables™. Doing something unexpected for a client builds solidarity and trust, especially if it meets a need. Through cooperative behavior and preparation, a win/win solution can be attained (see Figure III.1.c).

Let us illustrate this using a modern negotiating experiment we conducted in Ecuador with 350 participants negotiating virtually via internet. This role play involved a multiple-issue negotiation between a manufacturer and a service provider. We analyzed negotiation scripts from 175 participant pairs using the Hierarchical Individualized Limit Conjoint Analysis (HILCA) model of Drs. Markus Voeth and Uta Herbst of the University of Hohenheim, Germany. We inferred from the scripts that moments of tension were created due to the following reasons.

1) There was a lack of preparation by both parties,
2) Case understanding was poor by both parties,
3) The negotiation wasn't face-to-face,
4) Participants were in a hurry to finish the DEAL,
5) Some of the participants exercised a hard ball style without empathy, or
6) There was asymmetry in the negotiation (either in preparedness, understanding, or willingness to cooperate).

Each party's total fiscal responsibility in this multi-issue role play was tallied, so that negotiations could be classified as win/win (balanced) or win/lose (disparity). Most of the negotiations in this experiment ended with a win/lose negotiation outcome. In the win/win outcomes, we inferred from the scripts that one side was prepared and helped to walk the other side through the DEAL successfully. There were also scripts where knowledge was used as leverage to gain significant advantage.

Why were there so many win/lose outcomes? In this multi-issue negotiation, there appears to have been too much focus on commodity price and less attention on intangibles, which also carry significant value.

The great thing is to know when to speak and when to keep quiet

Seneca the youngest

TraDEAbLes™

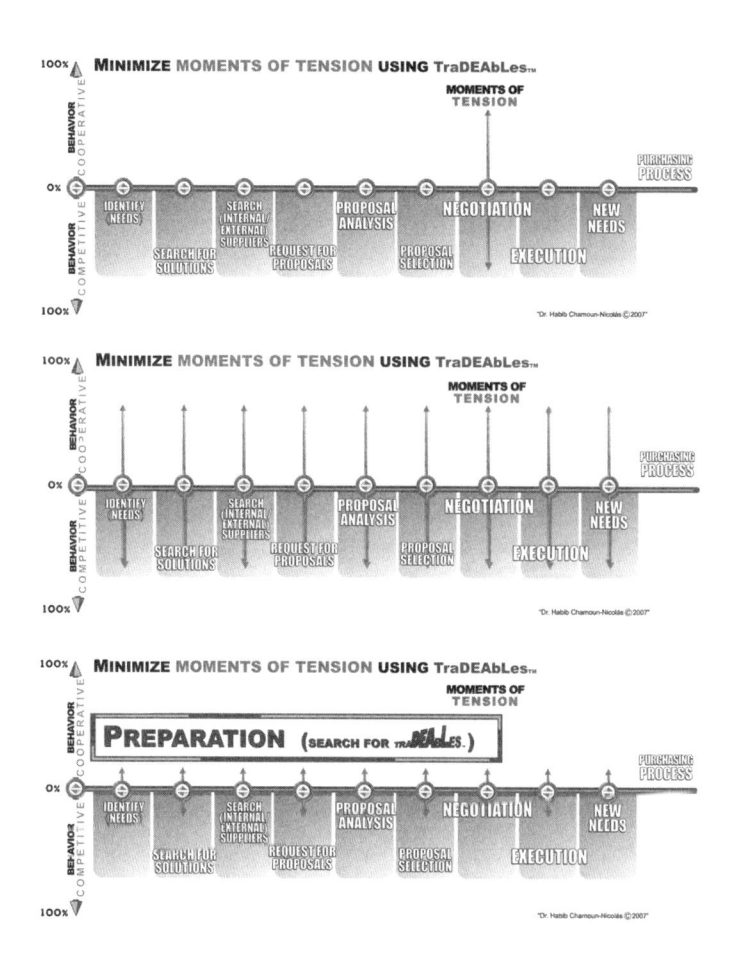

Figure III.1. Moments of tension during the sales process caused by cooperative and competitive behavior combinations: (a) tension arising at the point of negotiation, (b) tension at any point, and (c) tension reduction through use of Tradeables™.

Anecdote with Multiple Moments of Tension

I once received an honorary award in a foreign country. I had visited this country several times before without needing a visa. On the eve before the event, I flew from Houston to New York and on to my destination without a single request to see a visa.

At the country's first port of entry at 5 a.m. the day of the award ceremony, the immigration official reviewing my documentation said I was missing a tourist visa to entry the country. There was no way to get a visa issued that early in the morning. I faced deportation. The procedure in this country was to return passengers with no visa to the airline carrier for prompt return on the next available flight. The only authority in the country to issue a visa was the Secretary of External Affairs. I was directed to be back in the gate to board the 7:00 a.m. flight back home to the USA.

That was a moment of tension for me. It did test my negotiation skills, knowledge, and faith in God. I needed to find a way to stay and receive my award. After all, to receive an honor before high level dignitaries was a once in a lifetime event. I had information on alternate flights scheduled to depart the same day. There were only two options: the 7:00 a.m. flight through New York or a midnight direct flight to Houston.

I needed to prepare for the negotiation, knowing my goal and alternatives, if any. I determined that I needed to negotiate with two different decision makers: the immigration officials and, separately, with the airline representatives. My initial goal was to gain time – staying at the airport as long as possible. That goal could only be accomplished with the immigration officials. A second goal was to get the airline to agree to put me on the later flight, if I was unable to get a visa, and keep my original departure itinerary, a next day flight, if I successfully secured the entry document. My ultimate goal was to regain possession of my passport and get a visa from the Secretary of External Affairs.

Persuading the immigration officials to hold me in the airport until the second flight out would give me time and opportunity to call my local contacts and request assistance for a visa from the Foreign Affairs Secretariat. Second, I needed to mention that my visit to their country was to receive an honor, and it was a situation of take it or leave it. In other words, if I gained time at the airport, both immigration and I have nothing to loose and a lot to gain. I would gain the opportunity to receive the award, and they would have the satisfaction of helping someone their country wished to honor. I asked the highest immigration official at the airport early shift what was the longest time, according to procedure, for a non-visa visitor to remain in the airport.

He replied, "Maximum 12 hours."

I requested, "Could you please let me stay for that length of time, and could I call an official at the institution to ask them for help on issuing the visa?" I emphasized the importance of the event to my career. He replied affirmatively, but contingent upon airline carrier acceptance, schedule, and seat availability.

In private, I explained the situation to the airline official, and they accepted only because they had an available midnight flight. However, they were skeptical of my chances of getting a visa. There were two recent deportation cases: a Christian singer who was forced to cancel his concert and a Spaniard diplomat who failed to get timely issue of the document.

I located my contact by phone, and after only two hours of waiting at the airport, I got the tourist visa. The airline representatives were shocked. I tried to reason why I was successful where others were not. Did they request the extra time? Did they get mad and yell at the immigration officials? Did they blame the airline carrier? I don't know, but preparation, patience, perseverance, flexibility, and faith can guide you through a similar situation. Holding to the Phoenicians principles of respect and tolerance while peacefully working out differences helps beyond measure. Navigate around those moments of tension with clear goals and a good attitude.

TraDEAbLes™

The most important lessons learned were:

1. Never lose site of the negotiation objectives,
2. Know the key players to help accomplish those objectives,
3. Don't be afraid to state your case,
4. Be calm and flexible,
5. Don't blame anyone for your own mistakes,
6. Take one negotiation at a time and plan the sequence,
7. Have courage and faith in your actions,
8. Be prepared with options and alternatives for both sides,
9. Talk to decision makers; Avoid decision blockers, and
10. Create Tradeables™ whenever possible, even if it is simply being courteous in situations where people commonly are not.

Shallowness is natural; conceit comes with education.

Cicero, Pro Flacco

Tradeables™ Case Studies

Let's start by identifying the Tradeables™ in the following cases. In many DEALS, Tradeables™ are obvious, while in others, they may be more subtle and difficult to identify. Actions, thoughts, and concepts that ultimately leverage a DEAL are less tangible than a product or service satisfying a customer need outside of your product and services. Recall, we defined "Tradeables™" to be outside the scope of work of your actual DEAL. "Tradeables™" are creative solutions that satisfy other needs external from the ongoing customer negotiation.

On the other hand, if what are clearly Tradeables™ became the industry standard, they lose leverage capacity. For instance, I am in an ice cream store purchasing a double dip cone of pralines and cream. After a few licks, both scoops roll off and onto the floor. Immediately, the store attendant offers me another cone free of charge. The incident passes the test for Tradeables™; however, if this becomes an expected business practice, it loses all leveraging capacity, ceasing to qualify as Tradeables™. If the attendant does not offer a replacement ice cream, but I fully expected it as the norm, I could even become resentful and angry. Wow, Tradeables™, or rather lack thereof, can be converted into moments of tension. No replacement cone is simply a failure to meet expected levels of service.

When looking for Tradeables™, keep in mind that they are not always tangible items. There are times when old fashioned charm is able to penetrate the thick skin of a difficult negotiator and generate empathy for a fruitful business environment.

Let's analyze five negotiation cases involving Tradeables™:

1) Retail store negotiation,
2) Real estate negotiation,
3) Professional services negotiation,
4) Negotiations in advertising,
5) Fundraising negotiation

1) Retail Store Negotiation

While driving to the airport one day, I was explaining to my wife, Marcela, the Tradeables™ concept. She replied, "That concept may be applicable to the purchasing experience I just had. I bought a helmet and skates for my nephew, and after I paid and was ready to leave the store, the young salesperson offered five stickers free of charge to me. He commented, 'Your nephew will love the stickers.' The stickers were a dollar each, but I got them free." To Marcela, this was a great DEAL. She was happy, and anytime she will need something related to skating, she will no doubt return to the same store and the same sales person. This action of the salesperson shows us clearly the concept of Tradeables™.

Future sales were leveraged by the salesperson in giving away those stickers to Marcela. This would have been entirely different if before Marcela purchased the helmet and skates, the sales person said something like, "Mme, if your purchase is more than $50 dollars, I will give you five free stickers." In that situation, the sticker offering would have been a *Trade-in* or *Trade-off*. A salesperson saying, "If you purchase more, I will give you something extra," is not a case with Tradeables™, where the sole intention is to create leverage for present or future negotiations outside the present scope of the business DEAL.

As an afterthought, a moment of tension would have been presented by the sales person if he had included the stickers as an extra reduced cost item, thereby increasing the potential sales ticket. By creating a Tradeable, the sales person doesn't introduce any unnecessary tension.

2) Real Estate Negotiation

In the final process of purchasing a new home, a couple goes through an exhausting process with ups and downs and a myriad of small details – moments of tension. Seldom are food items included in a move, so the new homeowners find themselves with an empty refrigerator and a bare pantry. Consequently, a common situation in the first days of moving into the new house is the inability to cook a warm meal. Many couples prefer to eat at home in order to get over the moving stage as quickly as possible. In most cases, the

TraDEAbLes™

real estate broker, so helpful to the couple up to closing, has already made his own DEAL, garnered his commission, and completed his responsibilities.

Imagine that a real estate broker makes a surprise visit to the new house while a couple is in the moving stage and brings a large ice cooler full of orange juice, bottled water, soft drinks, fresh fruit, and assorted cheeses. This embodies the concept of Tradeables™. Similar to the skates case, the seller (broker) is providing unexpected actions that result in great surprise to his customer after the DEAL was consummated, leveraging future DEALS. While this couple may not be ready for another move within 4-5 years, the broker knows that personal recommendations can go a long way in this business. The broker had no official duties after selling the house, apart from value added actions. The broker knew of other client needs, such as what would make those first moving days smoother for his customer.

These two cases demonstrate that even in ordinary, day-to day negotiations, we can apply the Tradeables™ concept. It should be obvious that the "food need" was outside the scope of the work – the purchase of a new home. Those other needs being satisfied generated the Tradeables™ that could be of use in future negotiations.

3) *Professional Services Negotiation*

A client hired a consulting firm to develop a skillful and well prepared team of sales people. In the process of designing a sales program, the client asked the consultant if he knew a company that leased industrial equipment. The client was well aware that this activity was outside of the consultant's scope of services. It was more of a "favor" that was requested.

The industrial equipment that the client needed was very specialized and not commonly available on the market. It needed to be ordered at least 3 months in advance from a known source. The client had recently won a bid from a very prestigious corporation and needed to have the equipment within a 3-week window or face a penalty of $1000 per day – a moment of tension.

Coincidentally, the consultant knew an executive in a corporation that leased similar equipment on short notice. After an extensive search, the corporate representative located the desired equipment in idle use only a few hours away from the proposed jobsite. The equipment needed some maintenance and retrofitting, but it could be available in only a few days for delivery to the new site.

The client leased the equipment from the referred corporation, and the consultant solved his client's dilemma, even though it was only a "favor" outside of the services of the consultant firm. The consultant didn't receive any direct compensation beyond the sales

TraDEAbLes™

team development deal. Such actions are Tradeables™. The consultant increased leverage for future work with not only his client, but also with the corporation, since he initialized contact for a new revenue stream. This is not an example of *you scratch my back, and I'll scratch yours*. The good faith action from the consultant resulted in a work increase for the consultant with his initial client, and when the corporation was looking for someone to design and implement a business development program for their sales force, the consultant would have an inside track.

This case illustrates how Tradeables™ can produce win-win negotiations for all parties involved. The client avoided penalty and started his contract with the prestigious firm on the right foot, the corporation found a new use for old equipment and a new lessee, and the consultant obtained leverage for future work from multiple sources. This is, as are all these examples, a real case history.

4) Negotiations in Advertising

In the supermarket and convenience store business, negotiating shelf and display space with food and beverages suppliers is commonplace. All store space is not created equal! Store space varies on importance, with a premium on proximity to the incoming customer and to the registers. These are designated as first positions. Still, it's not just where, but also how much space is allowed per product line that matters. How well located and how much space a product occupies are important factors in sales and, thus, in the negotiation of space.

The food and beverage suppliers' negotiation priority is to position their product in what they called the house of the product (on the shelves) and also in the first positions. There are other spaces called "additional positions" that come as a second priority.

The *SupplyAll* food and beverage company, in an effort to negotiate space in a supermarket chain, sent a merchandiser to accomplish a goal of positioning product "X" on first positions as well as additional ones. The *SupplyAll* merchandiser first examined a particular supermarket in that chain where products "X" were already located. Firsthand inspection revealed that product "X" was only located at the "house of the product". The merchandiser then decided to negotiate with the supermarket manager for additional space, specifically in the first positions, especially at the registers.

Knowing supermarket managers are exceptionally busy, the merchandiser called for an appointment during a known slower pace portion of the sales day. Upon his arrival, the merchandiser greeted the supermarket manager and requested information on overall satisfaction and business concerns. The merchandiser listened to what the manager had to say rather than launch into the negotiation he had in mind. In the process of listening, the merchandiser found potential Tradeables™.

The manager mentioned that he felt the supermarket needed to have something to attract kids, and his goal was to increase product sales related to kids, including product "X". Kids were this supermarket's most valuable customers, and merchandise was simply not moving – a moment of tension. The merchandiser envisioned a possible attractor – a big, three dimensional display with toys. He shared his idea to attract kids with the manager, knowing that it could lead to increased sales not only of his company's product "X", but also competitors' products. The manager liked the idea and requested the merchandiser to implement it.

Considering additional client needs to increase their business, even if directly unrelated to the merchandiser's negotiation objective, gave leverage and increased the negotiation capacity to obtain more than expected. That is what Tradeables™ is all about. In the end, the merchandiser implemented the toy display to the manager's satisfaction. On the next visit, the merchandiser was able to upgrade the positioning of product "X" throughout the store. The merchandiser also found it easier to position his company's other product stock-keeping units (SKUs) all through the supermarket chain.

5) Fundraising Negotiation

A consultant was hired by a prestigious university with the objective to negotiate with potential sponsors to create an information technology research center.

After several months of courting potential sponsors for the research center, a group of university professors thought it prudent to contract a consultant to negotiate with the sponsors and close the DEAL. The consultant paid to negotiate the DEAL between the university and Fortune 500 company sponsors found Tradeables™ to be key in getting the DEAL done.

On the initial visit to potential sponsors with select faculty members, the consultant noticed that the decision-makers in this organization loved to play golf. The consultant asked the key executives if they played often. The response was that they didn't play as often as they wished. The executives often were able to close their own business deals on the golf course. Their competitors seemed to have no problem closing big deals, but they were – a moment of tension. The decision-makers verbalized their wish to become members of the city's most exclusive country club. In fact, 80% of the conversation on that first visit turned out to be about the game of golf. Before his departure, the consultant suggested that he could inquire about corporate membership openings, though he could not promise anything.

The professors that accompanied the consultant on this first visit to negotiate the funds for the research center were quite confused in that the majority of conversation centered on the game of golf and not about the sponsorship. The only outcome of the first visit in their view was a statement that the sponsors were willing to participate in the research center, only they needed time to check on their annual budget. The professors were very disappointed, because they wanted to have a rough dollar estimate of the sponsors' contribution. The consultant ensured the professors that the visit was a successful one despite an interpreted lack of progress toward the goal. Tradeables™ were identified. Even though Tradeables™ are exercised without expecting anything in return, the ground is fertile for future business dealings.

The consultant promptly inquired of corporate membership openings at the country club. The country club manager indicated a recent corporate membership cancellation – a rare occurrence. With a potential opening for a new corporate membership in the balance, the consultant brokered a meeting between the sponsor and the country club manager to discuss terms of corporate membership. There were no finders' fees for this action. Tradeables™ in this case simply involved the legwork leading to country club membership. Within two weeks the sponsors made the decision to fund 2/3 of the research center budget. At the grand opening, the president of the sponsor corporation wanted to meet the consultant that helped them get a country club membership.

Summary

- Tradeables™ are concepts, things, or actions that build negotiation capacity and momentum by satisfying client needs outside of our line of products or services.

- Tradeables™ are "favors" that sellers or buyers perform without expecting anything in return but are often key to the enrichment of our negotiation outcomes.

- Sometimes we need to satisfy client needs that have nothing to do with our scope of negotiation.

- Tradeables™ help leverage negotiations, creating trust and fostering long-term relationships.

- It seems as if moments of tension are the antithesis of Tradeables™.

Be careful about starting something you may regret
Syrus, Maxims

Chapter IV. Tradeables™: How to Produce Them

Phoenician silver stater with war galley
Arados mint, c. 350 BCE
Courtesy of Joseph Sermarini
http://www.forumancientcoins.com

Case studies, short stories, and anecdotes

We are going to review steps to create Tradeables™ and make a DEAL, in the style of the Phoenician masters. While it is highly recommended to apply a methodology in making any DEAL, Tradeables™ are the elements that we believe make the difference between a DEAL and a NO-DEAL.

Step 1. Understand before being understood

Phoenician example: In response to King Solomon's letter, King Hiram acknowledged receipt of the prior correspondence and echoed the request for clarity. Solomon spoke openly with Hiram of his divine mission, and Hiram replied, *"I have received the message you sent me and will do all you want in providing the cedar and pine logs."* Then he proceeded to tell King Solomon the specifics of how this need would be met. Knowing the purpose of the client, Hiram was able to deliver the quality product required.

Misunderstanding leads to unmet needs

Sometimes we embark into a fight without understanding how we got there to begin with. We don't listen to the other party, and we speak so loudly that we don't even hear ourselves. More than a month in advance of one of my conferences, I requested the event organizer to have a square wooden base for the cameras that would be recording my conference. The only specification was the height of the base could be 40, 50 or 60 cm high. Upon my arrival the eve before the event, I noticed there was no base whatsoever. I proceeded to the organizers booth for an explanation. The event organizer mentioned how he had called all over and couldn't find a square based that measured 40x50x60 cm. All were longer and wider. I acknowledged that there was a misunderstanding. We didn't care about the length or width, but only about the height. Rather than arguing over fault, we first gained clarity over the problem and worked toward a solution – getting the square wooden base. We need to understand before being understood.

The ideal real estate broker

An ideal real estate broker is always prepared before visiting a client, knowing ahead of time his client's needs, market values, and the competitors. He also had a very clear picture of his career goals and how to align them with every real estate daily negotiation objective. In particular, he should have answers to the following questions.

- ☑ What do I want to do with real estate properties – sell, buy, lease, or a combination?
- ☑ In what real state sector do I want to become specialized – industrial, residential, or commercial?
- ☑ What kinds of properties do I want to represent?
- ☑ Do I want to represent the seller, the buyer, or both?
- ☑ What type of customers should I target to reach my objectives?
- ☑ Do I have a structured plan to meet these objectives?
- ☑ And much more …

How can we increase our ability to understand? Here are six tips to improve this skill.

1.1 Listen without loosing goal clarity

Customers in the real estate business have many different needs. In fact, a customer wanting to lease a house, an office, or an industrial warehouse instead of purchasing may have very different needs and motivators to do so in contrast to one interested in purchasing. We can always guess why and fail, or we can simply ask.

We have repetitively observed real estate brokers not listening to but rather giving sales speeches to clients. They fail to understand what is it that the customer really wants and why they have chosen purchasing vs. leasing. Whether the salesperson is passionately convinced one method is superior or his motivation is driven by commission rate, he only frustrates the customer who comes with a predetermined set of needs.

Some common real estate customer needs are:

- Investment with business proposes,
- Space need for either industrial warehouse, residential, or commercial,
- Built to suit need or tailored made project need,
- Leasing a property for an income tax write-off,
- Expansion, growth need, and
- Company downsizing, divestment, or contraction.

TraDEAbLes™

A real estate broker trying to push his own listings on a client to maximize his commission is wasting his time stressing investment value to a client interested primarily in a tax break. The need to listen to the client is further reinforced with the following example.

A client wanted to lease ten industrial warehouses in ten different cities in a foreign country. The business objective was to increase product positioning throughout the 10 most important sites countrywide. A speed-to-market need was apparent. The existing warehouses didn't satisfy the short term client needs. The option of building warehouses to suit-the-needs simply took too long before an impact could be realized. Also, building in a foreign country takes even longer than the equivalent construction project in the USA due to unexpected surprises and hidden factors, such as land ownership issues, permitting, and governmental idiosyncrasies.

The broker helping the client to develop his business needed to generate options to satisfy the short and long-term client needs. By listening to his client without loosing sight of the goal the broker solved the problem. He accomplished this by asking enough questions to understand the needs and carefully listening to the responses. Only when he understood the client's reasoning was he able to truly propose a targeted solution. The alternative would have been to work up multiple scenarios until finally hitting upon one which worked – a very inefficient and frustrating experience for all. The broker proposed signing a short term lease on 10 different warehouses, which would allow positioning the product in the market fast enough, and building, in parallel, 10 warehouses with the specs the client needed to address long-term needs.

An old training rule attributed to noted author and motivational speaker Zig Ziglar applies: *No one cares how much you know until they know how much you care.*

1.2. Search for points in common

Many times we focus on the points in which we disagree instead of the ones we agreed upon. Although the broker saw clear advantage in a build-to-suit option, he decided to focus with his client on his urgent speed-to-market need. Consequently, he found a solution that was viable for the short term in the 10 warehouses case. Rather than trying to persuade the client to re-evaluate his needs assessment, he realized any approach which failed to address the recognized time-to-market need was not a solution. A short term lease agreement was obvious to both of them as meeting this immediate need.

1.3. Ask open and closed questions

The key to understanding the client needs in the above case was due to the broker asking many questions. Among the questions could have been:

- ☑ What size of warehouse are you looking for?
- ☑ What type of utilities and services do you like included in the warehouse?

TraDEAbLes™

- ☑ Are there any special precautions in storing your products?
- ☑ Are there restrictions or norms for your products?
- ☑ Do your products require a cool storage?
- ☑ Does every warehouse need an office?
- ☑ If so, how many people will work on the office?
- ☑ How many people will work in the storage warehouse?
- ☑ How do you transport the product?
- ☑ What type of trucks deliver the product to the warehouse?
- ☑ Do they need special opening in the warehouse?
- ☑ What about parking spaces?
- ☑ Why do you need so many warehouses?
- ☑ How soon do you need it?
- ☑ Why do you prefer leasing instead of purchasing?

This type of questioning helped the broker to design the spaces in the warehouse according to the client's needs, similar to the way an architect designs a house based on family needs. Asking enough questions early in the process not only leads to an improved understanding of your client's needs, but it also can identify Tradeables™ that satisfy other needs.

1.4. Use humor

Initial data from the client is often difficult to obtain. The key to any good information interchange is not just asking questions, but the answers must be reliable. A degree of comfort and trust is required. Sometimes the awkwardness of the situation is diffused by breaking the ice. One of the most ancient techniques to break the ice is using humor. Laughter generates good chemistry across all cultures.

1.5. Avoid prejudging

Stereotypes create barriers and often lead us to a reduced set of options. While it is important to understand cultural norms when doing business with those outside of our circle, avoid prejudging or supplementing fact for lack of information. We deal with people. If we remain flexible and give others the benefit of the doubt, we can negotiate much better. The Phoenicians were primarily in the business of cross-cultural negotiations and excelled at it.

1.6. Discover what motivates the other party?

What is good for the goose is good for the gander. Right? Well, this might be true of water fowl, but people have different motivational needs. Consider a job promotion. Some may only care about the salary increase, while others would be equally content to get the new and improved title without any significant jump in compensation. Power, respect, and perks can be equally potent motivators. In residential real estate, it is extremely important to find out what is it that motivates both the buyer and the seller, as illustrated in the following home sale case.

The house was on the market for nearly a year. Over that time there were several offers varying from $130,000 to $180,000. The owners, however, wanted at least $200,000 and were reluctant to sell at any price below the $200,000 anchor.

The house was appraised at $210,000, but the past two years have been a buyers' market, meaning that there were too many properties for sale with the prevailing demand for existing homes. There were recent indications that the economy was on an upswing, and the house value was forecasted to increase another 10% per year. After months of frustration, the broker asked the family why they were unwilling to undercut their selling price. He found out their motivation was purely a return on investment. They wanted to either sell the house and invest the money or lease it for a couple of years to capture the increased house value.

Knowing the real motivators, the broker was able to rent the house within weeks. Had the broker known the sellers' motivation earlier, the house would have been generating income for an extended period. The moral of the story is that knowing the real motivator of either the seller or the buyer makes it so much easier to satisfy client needs.

Step 2. Know the other party's 'rituals'

> Phoenician example: King Hiram wrote to Solomon, "*I am sending you Huram-Abi, a man of great skill, whose mother was from Dan and whose father was from Tyre. He is trained to work in gold and silver, bronze and iron, stone and wood, and with purple and blue and crimson yarn and fine linen. He is experienced in all kinds of engraving and can execute any design given to him.*" In this correspondence, Hiram demonstrated knowledge of the kinds of materials and skills required to build the temple and construct utensils for Hebrew worship.

I was in an African country in the middle of a downtown marketplace looking for souvenirs. I found a tiny antique store with beautiful wood sculptures and other exotic materials. It was a unique store with specialty items; you can't find these extraordinary pieces of art anywhere in the world but in this tiny store.

I was particularly attracted to two mahogany wood figurines. I ask the attendant for a price per piece. He responded $45 US per piece. He looked at my non-verbal expression and whispered in my ear, "We can make you a Deal if you have the intention to purchase." I walked the store looking for other items, but I refocused my attention on the figurines. I asked the owner what his best price will be. The owner, a tall, old, distinguished man, looked at me with an

TraDEAbLes™

intimidating stare. He didn't want to verbally respond to my request. He used his pocket calculator and showed me the result. This was a mute negotiation process – a ritual for this marketplace. The parallel to the silent negotiation of the Phoenicians is unmistakable.

Entering this silent negotiation, I requested his calculator to make a counter offer. I showed him my calculator result, $39 US for both pieces. He looked at me and smiled as if saying, "Are you crazy?" I smiled back and turned to walk out the door when he said, "Wait, wait, I can make you a Deal, $42 US for both pieces!"

"Sorry, I love the pieces, but I have only $39 dollars in my pocket, so it seems that we won't have a Deal today," I reluctantly replied. We actually reached an impasse. He wanted to sell but wouldn't; I wanted to buy and couldn't. The Deal collapsed, because I didn't have the ridiculous amount of $3 US in my pocket. I had a reasonable negotiation outcome without the means to meet the terms. The owner also was going to make a bad transaction if he accepted $39 US. I stepped outside the store and miraculously found an additional dollar bill. Immediately I returned saying, "I got your $40." Everyone in the store laughed except the owner, who perhaps thought I was bluffing.

I got a very cold, "No, I am not willing to sell at that price." The business environment had changed. Now it was public. His negotiating ego was at stake, and I felt offended by the crowd's reaction. I wouldn't dare make a counter proposal if even possible, and I walked away. I greeted all in the store upon my departure.

Later, while still downtown, I came up with three more wrinkled dollar bills from another pocket. I was not happy going home without any souvenirs and really liked those art pieces. I asked myself, "Should I care more about my ego, or should I go back to the store and try to close the Deal?"

I went back to the store and paid the man $43 instead of $42. I felt better paying an extra dollar, because the negotiation was not about the money, it was about principle. I was trying to get a Deal within a budget constraint. The owner was trying to get a Deal a few dollars over the cost. I knew this was a win/win situation. The owner got a dollar more than he wanted. I got a fair price, two pieces for $43 initially valued at $90.

Many people don't ask or even bother negotiating a Deal, even when it is customary. Know the other side's "rituals" and enter the process. Become equal without offending. Negotiate using good-faith principles and honesty guidelines.

2.1 Watch for habits and behaviors of the other side

Business transactions involve people. Often business deals cut across all cultures and personality profiles. For example, a good real estate agent is able to

TraDEAbLes™

empathize with the client and avoid confrontations due to differences of behavior. This is a little deeper than merely understanding the client's needs. It brushes upon the reasoning behind the need. Sometimes it's cultural. Sometimes it's personal. Sometimes observations hold our only clues.

With a globalized world that we live in today, almost every big city contains a microcosm of diverse cultures and traditions. When doing business internationally, we know we will encounter cultural norms different from our own. It is anticipated, and, hopefully, incorporated into our business approach. The astute businessperson must use the same caution when cutting across cultures within our domestic melting pot. Even within the same ethnic cultures, yet exposed to different environments, people behave differently to the same situations. We encourage all to observe more closely the "rituals" of the other party to be more successful in obtaining the desired negotiating outcome.

Let's compare and contrast American labor culture with Mexican labor culture in an isolated case study. It may shed some light on how to deal with these differences. A word of caution, it is not wise to generalize or create stereotypes from this specific case.

Business etiquette in the USA is to have a quiet, silent work atmosphere. There are, however, always exceptions to the rule. My first observation in an Anglo-dominated work environment was that my peers were doing their job from 8 a.m. to 5 p.m. in a very silent mode.

My first impression was very depressing, especially coming from a noisy work environment culture. In carrying out my work in the USA, I initially behaved as I had always done in Mexico. I was outspoken and loud. Others were complaining when I spoke on the phone with clients with my office door open. Apparently, I annoyed everyone within vocal range. I didn't know back then. In my culture, it was okay to be outspoken and loud. Being quiet was very uncomfortable. I began closing my office door so that I could continue to conduct business in the style to which I was accustomed. Occasionally, I would forget.

One day, the office manager suggested that I speak more softly and be more conscious of my surroundings. That day I learned to act and behave according to our natural environment, and when we change environments, we better adapt. The work environment is often non-negotiable, so we must negotiate with ourselves for the sake of producing a friendly and productive work ambience.

I was open and flexible to change those things that neither diminished my self-esteem or my dignity, nor enhanced my ego. In a different setting, I am always willing to change to make a happier environment for everyone. After all, negotiating is all about adjusting to what is important for others while maintaining what is essential to us.

2.2 Equal without offending

Observing the habits and traditions of the other party and mirroring or imitating is a good technique to follow. Beware of using this technique to such an extreme that it can be offensive, as opposed to creating empathy. The opening anecdote in this section employed this principle.

2.3 Understand the habit without prejudging

A typical "lost in translation" negotiation happened with two people from different cultures. As pointed out in my book, *Deal*, different cultures have different sensitivity to time. For the sake of simplicity, let's identify *high sensitivity to time* with being on time and *low sensitivity on time* with being late.

A client from a low sensitivity on time culture was looking to buy a house. A broker with a high sensitivity on time had an appointment with the client at 8:00 a.m. one day. The client arrived at 9:00 a.m. instead and repeated this behavior three times. The broker, in order to adapt to his client's culture, requested the next meeting at 8:00 a.m., and both arrived at 9:00 a.m. It can be argued that both were late, but this was a simple solution to a complicated and difficult situation. For some cultures being late connotes a lack of respect, and for others, it is a *modus operandi*. Find a way around differences rather than judging the actions of others with your own cultural yardstick.

2.4. Observe verbal and non-verbal signs

Sometimes non verbal messages can be a cultural barometer. Add the non-verbal to the verbal as suggested in the following example.

A broker was negotiating his fee with the owner of an industrial park. When the broker mentioned the standard commission rate to the owner, the expression on the owners' face indicated that the figure was on the high side. Rather than verbalize this, the owner became silent. The broker didn't pick up on this and was left clueless when the owner wouldn't return his calls to close the Deal.

When the negotiation turns to price, who should make the first offer? Most negotiation experts suggest you shouldn't give the first offer. While it may be best to wait for the other side to make an offer, what if the other party never gets around to it? Perhaps he has read this book also. As stressed in the book, *DEAL*, you must have a strategy and process in place. This section merely stresses that things almost never go as scripted. Be on guard for non-verbal communication and adapt to it. If you are unsure, ask.

Step 3. Prepare before responding (visit the store)

> Phoenician example: At the time when their Assyrian neighbors were aggressively subjugating their enemies, the Phoenicians examined their situation. They thought it wise to release some inventory to Tiglatpileser I rather than resist and face worse consequences. The 'kings of the seacoast' brought gifts of silver, gold, lead, copper, bronze, dyed wool and linen garments, an ape and monkey, wood, ivory, and even a dolphin, which Tiglatpileser I gladly received. Moscati spoke of the Phoenician preference *to "satisfy their powerful neighbors with homages and tributes."* The Phoenicians carefully sized up their situation, surmised the objectives of the other party, and chose the best business option available.

Many times we believe we know what the client needs and wants. We have a preconceived idea of what the client expects and wishes. However, a good rule of thumb is to *visit the store* before proposing in order to identify more opportunities. We use the term *visit the store* in a colloquial way, meaning visit your client's business, understanding deeply before proposing to discover other underlying non-apparent needs.

In Chapter III, we looked at a case study in supermarket product positioning. The supplier made an actual visit to a chain store to gather information that might prove useful in the negotiation. Let's accompany our merchandiser to the supermarket. Our main objectives on this visit are to locate our product, if there at all, and determine our goal – the space we'd like our product to occupy within the general layout of this store. With our objectives met, we feel prepared for our meeting with the manager at another location within the same chain. We arrive to the meeting site and immediately notice there are layout differences. Luckily, the manager was running late to our meeting, allowing us an opportunity to *visit the store* and reprioritize our product positioning goals. We thought we were prepared, but nothing replaces a look from within to make sure our negotiating objectives are valid and in line with what the client is able to offer.

In this step it is also good to find out what the expectations of the other party may be. Sometimes we oversell because we don't know that we have exceeded the client's expectations or undersell because we aim too low.

The same principles apply in any real estate deal. In hot housing markets, homes sell based upon internet bidding, site unseen. Often sales prices exceed the asking price. With a detailed description and ample pictures, this is possible. However, nothing replaces walking a property line, talking to neighbors, and seeing the property in its community setting to determine if the home satisfies all necessary criteria and merits the requested value. Most real estate agents will show a home in the absence of the owners. A *visit to the store* most credible is one where information is collected rather than spoon-fed.

3.1 Identify areas of opportunity

While *visiting the store* in the supermarket case, new areas of opportunity were found.

For the industrial site case in Step 1.1, the industrial broker ruled out areas of opportunity for different options while preparing and evaluating. Specifically, in some of the industrial parks visited:

- Parking space was deficient,
- The building wasn't built,
- There was no on-site office,
- The industrial site was far removed from rail transportation, and
- The industrial site was too remote for employee access.

Keep looking for new areas of opportunity and ruling out others. When on-site, new information is ripe for harvest.

3.2 Find the decision-making drivers

Once I was being filmed in a foreign country while teaching negotiation to a group of workshop participants. I was presenting new research materials from my work that were in the process of being published. I didn't notice the cameraman until the end of my talk. I told the organizers that I had not agreed to be filmed, and I needed to secure the original tape for copyright protection of unedited material not yet on the market. My driver was purely to avoid unedited material from getting to the public.

The organizers set up a meeting with the cameraman who immediately called his boss to explain the situation. As it turned out, the organizers had requested the cameraman to take pictures and film some event activities; however, the cameraman misunderstood and was filming the entire presentation with the intention to sell the material later to recover investment.

The cameraman's boss stated to the organizers that he always gets requests to film the entire events, and he didn't understand why this one was different. He needed to recover his investment, at least his cost for the cameraman's services and his transportation. He requested $100 to relinquish the tape. The organizer replied that their budget could only cover a $65 unexpected expense. They agreed upon the price, and I got the tape.

Later that same day, the organizers requested if they could keep the tape for their records. They promised not to make copies. I replied to the organizers, "I would hate to leave an unedited copy and risk that sometime in the future someone else will make copies and distribute the materials accidentally." The organizer argued that he needed the tape to support the expense and avoid misunderstandings. I responded, "If that is the case, I will pay you the $65, and everyone's problems are solved."

Every decision maker has a different motivator or driver. Mine was to get the tape as soon as possible to avoid distribution of unauthorized copies. The cameraman's driver was to get paid for the hours he had worked filming the conference. The boss needed to pay the cameraman and make a small profit. The organizer's driver was the need to justify the tape expense. Knowing the needs of every decision maker can diffuse moments of tension for everyone and get a better negotiating outcome.

3.3 Research pricing, but ask, "Is it worthwhile to renegotiate on price?"

Haggling is only a negotiation tactic and can be easily confused with the art of negotiating. There is a quantum leap difference between haggling and negotiating. Some people are proud of their haggling skills and call themselves great negotiators, because when the cake is cut, their portion is the lion's share. Every win for them is a potential loss for the other party. The purpose of haggling is to get the most out of any situation at any time. This is not negotiating. Here, we define negotiating as a problem-solving process to get the best solution for all – mutual gains. This is in direct contrast with haggling – a tactic used to get more and concede less. Haggling isn't inherently bad; it is a skill sometimes developed out of dire need, cultural risk, or game where reciprocity is not of concern.

While haggling and negotiating are not equated, every negotiation can incorporate some degree of haggling. In short-term relationships, haggling tends to appear more frequently. In a desire to foster long-term business relationships, haggling is a threat to the perceived good will of the parties. A tactic used to gain maximum advantage devalues relationship. A business partner who feels he is going into battle when approaching a negotiating table or a business lunch may opt for more congenial business relationships.

It is said that a good haggler is a good negotiator. Nonetheless, the best negotiator is the one that brings both parties to a winning table. Sometimes great negotiators give more than they receive in the short term to gain in the long term (Tradeables™). Haggling creates discomfort and, on some occasions, distrust among the parties, whereas Tradeables™ create trust and leverage the negotiation to a higher degree of relationship.

Industrial park options

A client was planning to establish an industrial plant in an industrial city. A broker helped him evaluate options and narrow the field to two choices. The most expensive option was located inside an existing industrial park with first class standards and norms. In the other option, an investor was going to purchase land, develop the site, and lease it to the client.

The first option was a 5-year lease contract which included maintenance and security services. The second one had no provision for maintenance or security, and the development was to be in an isolated part of town. The investor for the second option had no experience with industrial parks. The client in this second option needed to contract directly the security and maintenance personnel. This was a bigger risk due to a lack of experience of the developer and the possibility of complex labor relations in hiring maintenance and security services. It could easily be more costly in the long run.

Sometimes negotiating is not about haggling for the best price but finding the right solution. In this case, the client decided to go with the more expensive option, because saving money on the initial price was not the only consideration in making a DEAL. Haggling for a great price can block our global vision. Prepare to talk price, but enter such a negotiation only at the proper time with all other considerations appropriately weighted.

3.4 Search and know market standards and references

I recall an undeveloped field valued at only 10% of its present price 10 years ago. How clever for those possessing the vision (and capital) to purchase the field as an investment, resulting in a substantial margin. Perhaps the buyer had studied growth patterns and had suitable examples of land value appreciation in analogous cases. Many times we don't know how future events or external factors can influence the market price, but sometimes we can make reasonable estimates and use that information to make better business decisions. Create benchmarks and analogs when possible. Leverage your DEAL with such reference cases, particularly to support speculative ventures.

3.5 Determine expectations and aspirations of the party

A novice broker was shocked when he received his first real estate commission. The broker's expected to receive the standard 3% commission for helping to execute the purchase of a commercial building. Instead, only a fraction of the amount he thought was due to him showed up on his commission check. To the broker's surprise, his expected commission in this first transaction was shared with the owner's broker, the real estate firm, and his colleagues! His fraction would not cover both the bills and purchases he had already envisioned.

Know the rules. After the transaction is executed is not the time for discovery. Avoid negotiating based upon assumptions. Renegotiation is seldom an option. The other party may be negotiating with full knowledge of the ramifications. You know your expectations. Know the expectations of the other parties to make the best DEAL. If either party is disappointed in the outcome of any DEAL, it may affect future business prospects and long-term business relationships.

3.6 Know the needs of the other party

A newlywed couple wanted to lease a home in a city where central air conditioning was not standard. Homes there typically supported window units, but if you leased a home rather than purchase, you were expected to supply your own window A/C unit. The city was actually in a foreign country where air conditioning was optional due to the prevailing moderate climate, but having air conditioning was also a sign of socio-economic status.

The newlyweds had two A/C units as a wedding gift. In the early stages of the lease negotiation process, the husband proposed through the broker that the home owner purchase the A/C units from him to remain permanently with the house. Doing so would add value to the house and enable it to be leased more rapidly in the future.

Understanding both the broker's needs and the owner's needs, the husband signed a two-year contract and sold the units to the home owner. Everyone won in this negotiation. The owner leased the house and increased his property value and the home's marketability, the broker won by signing a lease contract sooner than expected, and the newlyweds received a cash windfall, plus the two-year benefit of air conditioning.

Knowing what would benefit other parties in the negotiation allows us to identify terms beyond the base transaction that add value to the DEAL for all.

3.7 Understand the negotiation objectives of the other party

At first glance, this appears to be covered in the prior tips about knowing the needs of the other party. However, just as the purchase of the A/C units was not an original negotiation objective of the homeowner, each party's needs are not always captured in their objectives. Earlier examples discussed different motivations for buying versus leasing. Objectives nearly always meet a perceived need. A great DEAL will not only capture each party's objectives, but it will also address needs that are not necessarily on the table. Recognizing and differentiating between needs and objectives allows Tradeables™ to be identified and used to make a good DEAL great. The incorporation of the A/C units into the home lease deal was not a Tradeable™. If the widow units had been offered outside the DEAL rather than sold as part of the DEAL, they would have been Tradeables™.

TraDEAbLes™

Step 4. Take time to plan your strategy

> Phoenician example: The Phoenician trading empire didn't materialize overnight. It took years, and perhaps generations, to see the fruit of colonization efforts and network building. Such undertakings require a sound strategy, the ability to accomplish the goal, and the determination to see it through. Going into a negotiation without due preparation would be comparable to Phoenician merchant ships simply meandering the seas with no cargo in search of buyers.

4.1 Don't rush the DEAL

Negotiating for retail fixed price items

I went with my brother to purchase a digital camera from one of the biggest retail electronics stores in the USA. He wanted a sophisticated digital camera that was on sale only for that week. Before entering the store, I asked my brother if he had a negotiating strategy to purchase the camera.

He replied, "What do you mean?"

I commented, "Do you know your goal in this negotiation? Do you know your walk away price? Do you know your best and worst alternative to a negotiated agreement? Are you prepared to buy it on the terms of the advertised sale?"

He answered, "Well, there is a discount already and a published Manufacturer's Suggested Retail Price (MSRP) reference value. There is not much we can do. Is there?"

I replied, "Hold on. Can you ask for an additional value-added item?"

He thought about it, then said, "I am planning to purchase a 2-gigabyte memory stick for added convenience. The unit comes with only 64 Mb."

I commented, "What about a leather case for the camera? Wouldn't it be nice to get it for free?"

"Oh, yes," he replied.

Then I asked, "What happens if everything goes according to plan? Should we take a break to see what bonus may be offered?"

We found the camera and the memory stick. All he was missing was a nice leather case for the digital camera. I asked him to be brave and ask the store attendant for a case as a bonus. He did.

The store attendant confidently rebuffed, "No, this store doesn't bundle giveaways on sale items."

I told my brother to be persistent and insist again.

After the second request, the store attendant replied, "I will ask the store manager, but it is doubtful the store manager will approve giving you anything for free." The store attendant passed along the request to the store manager, and to his surprise, my brother got a free leather case for his brand new digital camera.

Asking, persistence, and good attitude were keys to closing this DEAL with better terms than initially purposed. In retail purchasing, the consumer too often assumes that the terms are preset; however, nearly every store manager has some power of discretion, which may not rest with the salesman level. Planning a negotiation strategy prior to entering the store was a must.

Take time to evaluate options. As in comedy, timing is ever so important. People, in general, detest being rushed into making decisions. Applying time constraints applies pressure. Pressure can either push parties toward a DEAL or lead to a collapse in negotiations. Don't apply undue time pressure to your own decision-making unless the DEAL is the one for which you planned.

4.2 Take a moment before closing

The closing of a DEAL should be a point of tension release if the DEAL satisfies all objectives driven by needs. Never leave the table second guessing or being unsure of all the DEAL encompasses. A feeling of being cornered is not the preferred impetus for closing. Take time to gain clarity and understanding. At the same time you are running through your checklist of objectives and terms, the other party might interpret your hesitancy as a reluctance to close and sweeten the DEAL. Take a break and seal the DEAL with confidence.

4.3. Give a break to the other party

At a particularly sensitive portion of a negotiation to purchase an industrial facility, a customer requested to end the session with a broker and rejoin the next day. When the other party agreed, great relief was shared by all. When the session reconvened, the parties were able to progress smoothly through the negotiation with much reduced apprehension. Sometimes it makes sense to propose a recess, especially if the other side gives non-verbal cues that the process merits a fresh start. Sequestered juries often reach consensus by attrition. Don't accept less than a DEAL which will satisfy rather than suffice.

4.4 Don't pressure yourself

For some, working under pressure is exhilarating. For most, it is not. Negotiating under pressure increases the chances for mistakes, resulting in leaving money on the table for both parties. Negotiating without ample preparation automatically adds pressure to yourself.

Step 5. Propose solutions

> Phoenician example: The Phoenicians were known for fostering long-term business relationships based upon great products and fair deals. Recall in the cited writings of Herodotus, the Phoenicians were known for displaying their wares, allowing inspection of goods, and giving trading partners the opportunity to set a value. *"Neither party deals unfairly by the other: for they themselves never touch the gold till it comes up to the worth of their goods, nor do the natives ever carry off the goods till the gold is taken away."* A sense of fairness at the conclusion of any deal by both parties is nearly always a prerequisite for return business.

5.1 Don't over-estimate your position

Negotiating at the airport

At the airport, while waiting to board my plane, the airline attendant broadcast over the public address system, "We are oversold by one seat. If someone would volunteer to go instead on the next flight in two hours, we can give them a $300 voucher for future travel."

One passenger ran to the ticket counter and requested "Can you sweeten the DEAL? Could you do more? Could you place me in first class?"

The airline attendant replied, "Let me see what I can do."

Then another passenger approached and inquired, "Are you still looking for volunteers?"

She answered, "Yes, let me have your name in case we need to use your seat."

I was watching the whole interaction close by and commented to the second passenger, "Great DEAL, isn't it?"

He replied, "Definitely, 300 bucks on a voucher, you bet it is a great DEAL!"

On the plane, I saw both volunteers board as well. Although they volunteered, there was no need for their seats after all. The first volunteer was so demanding that he didn't even get a chance for consideration. Sometimes we need to get what is offered to us in the moment, without being so greedy or demanding, overestimating our position. Being too aggressive risks calling the DEAL off. The first volunteer overestimated his position in proposing additional terms which did not get him to a DEAL closing.

5.2 Fair solutions are the most appropriate

Multiple parties negotiating case

I was asked by a client to coach his personnel on conducting professional and ethical negotiations with their customers. My client was an insurance underwriter. Insurance companies have different layers of distributors, brokers, sub-brokers, etc. This case followed a particular negotiation between an insurance company representative, a regional insurance broker, and a potential reseller for the broker. The reseller had different sales points within the brokers' regional coverage. The broker was an independent who generated 10% of the sales for this insurance company's region. My job was to coach the insurance representative in negotiations with different regional brokers and their resellers.

In this particular exchange, I was playing the role of observer. The insurance representative and I prepared before visiting the broker and reseller. We planned to visit the broker first and then the reseller. We had predetermined the ground rules for the negotiations. The insurance company representative led the negotiations with both the broker and reseller. The main objective of this negotiation was to gain an enhanced position in the reseller's portfolio of insurance company products. The reseller had great potential to increase sales of these insurance products. The broker maintained both a personal and business relationship with the reseller, so the role of the broker was to break the ice and free the path for the insurance representative to conduct the negotiation.

The insurance company representative and I determined our negotiation strategy and goal, including, but not limiting to, setting commission ranges as a function of different insurance products and services, insurance duration, and coverage level. For example, commissions ranged from 25% to 51% for one insurance product and 25% to 28% for other products. These commissions were to be extended to the final reseller and included a small commission for the regional broker.

At the broker's office, the insurance company representative briefly discussed the plan we had prepared to negotiate with the reseller. The broker didn't agree with our plan. He suggested we offer an attractive proposal to the reseller up front.

We decided to first listen to the reseller, and depending on his needs, offer plan A, B or C. Plan A was clear and straightforward. If we ascertained that reseller didn't really know the products well, we would offer the lowest commission, 25%, as a base rate with incentive commissions based upon sales. Plan B was appropriate if the reseller was very competitive and had a great reputation in the industry. In this case, then we would offer a higher base commission with a sales-based cap on incentive commissions. If the meeting was going nowhere, Plan C called for postponement and meeting rescheduling.

At the reseller's office, we found out that he was relatively new in the business, so Plan A was most applicable. The broker did a great job breaking the ice, and the reseller was very impressed with the insurance company. It was exactly what he was looking for. The reseller wanted to diversify his business by representing the insurance company and selling insurance products to his captive market. He was a leader in his type of services, and selling insurance meshed well with his current offerings. The insurance company representative realized this reseller would make a good partner. He operated with multiple sales points and was a leader in his market, just with no experience in insurance products. The regional broker would be able to cover that weakness, and it sounded like a win–win DEAL.

In the middle of the conversation, the reseller requested information on commissions, terms, and conditions. At this point, the insurance company representative (an inexperienced negotiator) requested that the broker explain the range of commissions available to the reseller. Though we had prepared for insurance representative to be the lead, he delegated his negotiation leadership to the broker – a first mistake. The broker was also surprised. When he began giving examples of commissions (a second mistake), he cited the biggest base commission rate possible, setting up false expectations.

The broker also gave out wrong information (third mistake) while explaining the different commissions available for different products. He stated that commissions were computed on gross price and not the net. This, too, inflated expectations. The reseller immediately agreed to work with the insurance company and proceeded to questions concerning policy issuance and execution.

After leaving the office, I held a debriefing session with the insurance company representative and the broker. I stressed:

At preparation,

- Write the negotiation ground rules, and don't break them,
- Decide who is leading the negotiation,
- Understand each person's role,
- Have a strategy,
- If you need to change strategy, take a break.

While negotiating,

- Don't pass the leadership role unless aligned with strategy,
- Don't surprise your team members,
- Include the team in the preparation phase (to avoid and minimize risks),
- Do not procrastinate when you have a negotiation team and strategy,
- Correct mistakes instantly.

To be fair, I suggested that the broker call the reseller and admit his mistake. Get the terms straight before he has agreed 100% on selling the insurance products. It is better to be honest and straightforward with clients and correct mistakes as soon as possible. Don't deliver late term bad news.

5.3 Doubting your intuition is sometimes necessary

While the general belief is to listen to your gut feelings as a last minute resource, when negotiating in a situation with scanty data available, make an intelligent decision. If you are confident, challenge yourself with the facts of the case. If you are under-confident, avoid converting intuition into fact.

I remember negotiating with a client who stared down a salesperson on a store visit. Something amiss was obvious between these two individuals. During a requested break from this negotiation to sort out this problem, I learned that the client and this particular salesperson had a previous negative negotiation experience. My intuition to take a break was correct; otherwise, things would likely have gone awry. We figured out a way to minimize tension in this negotiation and get to a quicker DEAL by redefining the negotiating strategy.

5.4 Help the other to make the decision

I recall an old movie scene about relations between Mexico and the US. A young American lady was taking a cab to rendez-vous with her fiancée in Mexico City. He was a soldier coming back through the Panama Canal to Mexico City. That was the fashion; a lot of ladies would meet their fiancées in Mexico City to get married after the war was over. The young lady was getting out of the taxi when she asked the cab driver, "How much do I owe you, Sir?"

The cab driver replied, "$5 dollars, dear lady."

She answered back, "Oh mister, I only have a dollar left."

He countered, "Okay, three dollars."

She replied, "$2 dollars only!" to which they reached an agreement.

The cab driver was curious that such a nice looking, well dressed lady would be negotiating over price, so he questions her, "My dear lady, just out of curiosity, why did you haggle over price with me?"

To his surprise, she replied, "It is in the book." She pulls a guidebook out of her purse and shows it to the driver. She continued, "In this book, it says if a taxi driver asks for 'x' amount of money, you should offer half that amount."

Following the advice of the guidebook helped the driver to make a decision. However, negotiating 'by the book' doesn't always yield the book results. We need to be more creative and offer solutions. We cannot expect people to behave according to script. Be careful with stereotypes or prototypes. Having delivered this admonition, making a decision for your client is a must in cultures of indecisiveness.

TraDEAbLes™

Step 6. Accord

> Phoenician example: As documented in the historical accounts section in Chapter IV, the Annals of Tyre, though lost through the ages, were described as *"public writings, and are kept with great exactness, and include accounts of the facts done among them, and such as concern their transactions with other nations also..."* The Phoenicians knew that a good recordkeeping system was essential to keep the facts straight and the parties true to their word. It was and is simply good business.

6.1 Get your agreement in writing

A written ethical agreement was an excellent tool in the first business endeavor I had with my brother. It included what we had agreed upon and our roles and responsibilities on the given scope of work. It was more of a clarifying document than a legal one. It was clear and concise to avoid misunderstandings concerning our duties. It is not about mistrust when you write an agreement; it is about setting a clear goal and vision of what the relationship should be. Even with the most trustworthy and beloved member of your family, set it on writing. Surprisingly, this removes tension that might result from a blending of personal and business expectations.

This brings me to another quick anecdote. Not everyone has a good memory. There is a tendency to forget, especially if there are too many details involved. After negotiating a consulting fee with a client, I forgot to put in writing. The consulting job took longer than expected to kick off. After more than a year later, neither the client nor I could remember the agreed consulting fee. We had to start all over. To avoid situations such as this, put it in writing.

6.2 Write points in which agreement is reached and points excluded

In the previously described negotiation experiment conducted in Ecuador with 350 participants negotiating via internet, roughly 80% of the scripts documented the terms of agreement. In contrast, less than 5% of the scripts included points they didn't agree upon. We infer that it is easier for people to communicate what the scope of their future business will include but more difficult to mention what the scope is not. Simply, people assume what is not included. There is significant potential for moments of tension and conflict in the aftermath of a negotiation which fails to get agreement on what is not included in the DEAL. Perhaps this is related to the natural desire to accentuate the positive and downplay the negative.

In any negotiation, it is vital to write down what points in which we are in agreement and which ones we failed to produce an accord. We must be sure of what the agreement includes and what it doesn't. Be aware of what is not included in your contract.

TraDEAbLes™

Step 7. Verify

> Phoenician example: Again from the story of *First Contact Sales*, Phoenician trading vessels would display their wares and leave them for private inspection. The natives would leave a quantity of gold – a first offer. The Phoenicians would then inspect the initial offer. If insufficient, the cycle repeated. When this verification process concluded, each took their prize. In this example, each offer was clear and verifiable. There was ample opportunity for value adjustment and no chance of error concerning what was on the table (or beach) – only equitable deals closed.

7.1 An agreement without verification is potential for conflict

Negotiating a change of scope

On a Paris trip, we made a reservation through a US carrier to lease a large minivan that could sit six people and four large pieces of luggage. While picking up the car, I verified with the agent that it will sit six people comfortably and hold four large pieces of luggage. The vehicle we were given was indeed able to seat six, but there was not enough luggage space.

I went back to the very nice and polite French receptionist. I practiced my best French in explaining the situation.

She said, "Yes, Monsieur, this van will fit four large pieces of luggage, but not the US standard large."

Voilà, here was a negotiating opportunity. I politely explained my situation and why the van assigned did not meet my expectation. In the US, *large* is *large*, but in France, *large* is apparently a different size of *large*. This large wasn't large enough. I asked her if we could get a van size upgrade. She mentioned that there was a 9 passenger van that can fit six pieces of large luggage. I presumed that the space for six large luggage items was still less than required, but we could use the additional seating for storage. Then I asked her if I could get it for the same price because of the honest misunderstanding. After some discussion, she agreed to it. This was a great vacation.

Verification is important, and surprises are more possible when dealing cross-culturally. In this case, verification at the point of sale still did not reveal the failure to reach a mutually agreeable DEAL. There is always room to negotiate. When caught off-guard, quickly find options to solve your needs. Help the salesperson find an amicable solution. Point out clearly what your expectations were in the agreement. Sometimes when you feel short-changed, there are still opportunities to build your Tradeables™. Verification avoids conflict. When verification measures reveal a misunderstanding, we must renegotiate. With diplomacy and quick thinking, sometimes you can surpass your original goals.

7.2 Rethink the initial strategy

Negotiating an invaluable or valueless item

On a trip to Europe, my family and I visited antique stores to look for pieces of history. One of my kids, Antoine, was only 7 at that time. He was interested in antique watches. Antoine was fluent in Spanish and English and knew a few French words and phrases. We entered an antique store, and before we noticed, Antoine was in the back corner waiving his hands and negotiating a price with an old French lady. There was considerable gesture exchange.

As I got within listening range to his conversation, Antoine asks me, "Dad, how do you say in French, 'Lady what is your best offer?' I really want this watch but not too much."

In the end, Antoine and the old lady got what they wanted. Antoine purchased an antique watch that didn't work, and the old lady got a few Euros for something taking up space in the store.

I asked Antoine jokingly, "Why did you want an antique watch that doesn't work. Besides, there is no reference for the price. It is so old that you can say it is either worthless or priceless."

He answered, "Dad, this is art, and besides, I love it. I only paid a couple of Euros for it. None of my friends have one. It is unique."

I learned a lesson from Antoine. There are other motivators to purchase things. I let Antoine make his DEAL, but at the end of the negotiation, as a loving and concerned father, I asked both of them to state their agreement to verify the DEAL and avoid misunderstanding.

7.3 Verifying agreements helps avoiding renegotiations

Our research in cross-cultural negotiation, as documented in my book *DEAL* and elsewhere, shows that some cultures dislike verifying an agreement. This is true of the Mexican business culture. This avoidance is due partly to the fear of losing what we already have negotiated. As such, verification could be uncomfortable for your negotiating partner. By the same token, it is very likely that a renegotiation will be required if we don't verify.

Step 8. Execute

> Phoenician example: The deal King Hiram struck with Solomon was consummated to the satisfaction of all. The temple was built and dedicated in full adornment with items skillfully cast by Huram-Abi. Then there were palaces to be built. The business relationship spanned more than two decades. Each party met their obligations and exceeded expectations. The Phoenicians knew that execution of the first deal was not the end, but only the beginning of a business relationship.

8.1 Don't stop midway

I am amazed at the time and dedication business people spend on getting to a DEAL only to end up sitting in a courtroom due to lack of execution by one of the parties. What we promise is one thing; what we actually deliver is another. A great negotiator follows the seven habits of the Phoenicians and manages the DEAL to execution. Stopping midway creates moments of tension. A DEAL without execution is like a wedding that never gets to the honeymoon.

8.2 A lot of accords don't get to fruition because of lack of execution

Negotiating with a handy man

One day I called the insurance company to fix the refrigerator, the microwave oven, and the dishwasher, which were all covered under my homeowner appliance policy. The handyman fixed everything with the exception of the refrigerator. The freezer wasn't making ice cubes. The handyman told me the solenoid wasn't working, and the insurance policy didn't cover that part. I asked him if he knew where I could get the replacement part, where the solenoid was, and how to extract the defective unit, which the repairman was happy to do for me.

I purchased the solenoid and was ready to fix the problem myself. Though briefed, I was still fearful that I might break something or botch the installation. I telephoned the repair company for an estimate. I was told the job would cost $100, but it could take two weeks to schedule the house call. That was all the motivation I required. I managed to replace the solenoid in less than 15 minutes.

Sometimes risk inhibits our timely execution. I called to get a price, thinking cost was the bottleneck to a DEAL. As it turned out, two more weeks without ice cubes was too long for me. Negotiating is about problem solving, generating options, creating opportunities, and execution.

8.3 Good intentions are not a substitute for action

How many times has your son had the good intention to cut the grass in the backyard? How many times have your clients had the good intention to pay your work on time? How many times have you promised to be on time, on schedule, and deliver? How many times have we parents had good intentions to be home to celebrate a special occasion with our kids? How many times have husband and wife had the good intention to forgive one another? How many times do we fail to act? A good negotiator backs up his words with action. He is flexible, methodical, and open-minded towards alternate solutions.

Step 9. Confirming

> **Phoenician example**: The Tyrian business records were public. As such, anyone could request to review the historical logs. Recall the citation of Josephus from our Case Studies from Ancient Historians section where he said, "...*if anyone would know the certainty about [the letters between kings Solomon and Hiram], he may desire the keepers of the public records of Tyre to show him them, and he will find what is there set down to agree with what we have said.*" In this fashion, parties can verify terms and compare plan versus action.

9.1 The opera isn't over until the fat lady stops singing

Once I negotiated a great hotel rate for my family while visiting France. Since we are a large family, I had to book three hotel rooms near Paris. The rate that I negotiated was so incredible that I decided to confirm by e-mail with an attachment letter in French stating the agreed fare, which also included breakfast for all. Upon arrival, the hotel receptionist couldn't believe the fare that I got for the three hotel rooms. In fact, my total hotel rate was even lower than the average price for one hotel room. The receptionist couldn't find the letter I sent to the hotel, but I produced a copy of the letter in French that specified the family hotel rate and conditions.

TraDEAbLes™

Always make a written agreement, especially when doing business cross-culturally. An incredible DEAL is only incredible if the terms are honored. Written confirmation is good policy and good business.

9.2 An accord isn't an accord if is not confirmed in detailed

In home construction, the finish out is vitally important to making a house a home. Details should not be left out of an agreement, and every detail agreed upon should be considered important. Failure to pay attention to detail early often drags out the project, which can be bad for both parties. Confirm everything in detail before project execution.

It is better to trust in courage than in luck.

Syrus, Maxims

Chapter V. Tradeables™: A Phoenician Gift to You

Seaport with the Embarkation of the Queen of Sheba: Claude Lorrain, 1648. Oil on canvas, National Gallery, London.

Today, we live in a complex world where we are bombarded in the newspapers and on TV with conflicts in the home, at the office, in courts of law, and on battlefields around the globe. I am speechless watching senators and congressman fight over polarizing issues like boxers, pummeling each other with their fists. Similarly in other spectator sports, emotion at soccer matches takes precedence over reason, generating insane actions on and off the field of play.

In Phoenicians times, the world was also a dangerous place. The Phoenician business philosophy steered them through a period of rapid expansion and wealth amidst regional wars, coupes, and revolutions. Following the merciless pillage of Tyre by the Macedonian king, Alexander the Great, the Phoenicians no longer had a geographical center of power in history. However, their business practice of colonization and trade expansion dispersed the Phoenician heritage and culture throughout the populated world. The Phoenician identity and philosophy prevails even today.

I believe we are going through changes as profound as those of the Phoenician era. Alvin and Heidi Toffler mentioned on their latest book *Revolutionary Wealth*, "The third and latest wealth wave is increasingly based on knowledge – and puts economics back in its place as part of a larger system, bringing, for better or for worse, issues like cultural identity, religion and morality back towards central stage." We are observing extreme technological changes today, especially in computational power and communications. The Phoenicians embraced technology and put it into standard business practice, whether it was in glass manufacturing, metallurgy, or ship building. Such leverage of technology has encouraged some historians to link Phoenicians to Aztec, Mayan, and Inca cultures (Johnston, 1965). Whether the Phoenicians in their 3-year voyages upon the ships of Tarshish navigated amongst the islands of the Pacific all the way to the Americas is irrelevant to our position that the Phoenicians, as developers and guardians of advanced technology, integrated technology into their business model. Have we adequately harnessed the power of computers and communications to leverage our ability to construct win-win solutions in business, education, politics, and world affairs?

And what about working for the greater good? Are we so focused on self that we forget about the welfare of others? Recall life is but a vapor. Time is our ally and every-marching foe. Which depends upon your philosophy of life and whether that philosophy is backed by action. We must not forget the basic principles of human courtesy, respect and tolerance – even in business.

What is the solution for the negotiations of the future if we don't even agree on the basics of human interaction? Is the solution as simple as marching back 4000 years to learn from a proven, ancient business philosophy? A lost art of those Phoenician business principles involved the use of Tradeables™ – finding unmet needs of your trading partner and satisfying them outside the scope of a business deal. The rapport and trust gained from such practice is invaluable.

Some simply cannot see the value of giving something away. They see their negotiation party as a necessary adversary. He is needed for our current business, but we don't care about his business, whether he survives or not. They do not care to foster mutual long-term gain if short-term profit is in aim.

In business, we must preserve identity while respecting others. There appears to be an element of spirituality involved when we desire to enlarge our circle of caring into our business actions. Spiritually sensitivity has been identified as the number one newest trend for business in the coming decade (Aburdene, 2005). Tradeables™ embraces this spirit of fostering trust and business comradery.

I challenge you to study the beliefs and methods of the ancient Phoenicians. Make a change in your business philosophy, and negotiate like a Phoenician. I invite you to start today by training your kids to be better negotiators. Let me illustrate this with the following story.

The Next Generation

Modeling negotiation skills to your kids helps them develop the art of execution. An opportunity for people in sales is the execution of the DEAL. Too often sales people tend to promise things and don't deliver. Out of such grows the aura of the used car salesman.

Sometimes you only need to be yourself in executing a DEAL, getting more things than you expected from others. At a gift shop in front of the Eiffel tower in Paris, the owner of the store gave Marcelle, my youngest, an extra gift just because she was nice and smiled to her. My sons, Habib, Emile, and Antoine, are also good negotiators; it is a skill I've watched develop as they watch Marcela and me either preparing for a workshop or conducting daily life. Habib, my oldest son, once got extra bonuses all by himself while purchasing soccer game tickets. He got t-shirts for all with the signatures of the soccer team players. He only requested if the tickets included the t-shirts, and they gave them to him. Emile, my second, is also excellent at negotiating. He describes stories, sells ideas, and before you know it, he gets what he wants. Antoine, the youngest of the boys, showed his negotiating skills in the antique store negotiating case of Chapter IV.

Training your kids to become better negotiators should be of interest to every parent. However, if our kids see us conduct our life with a win-lose philosophy, they too will pattern that self-centered mode of interaction with the world. I have trained my kids to negotiate with facts and data, not just to get what they want, but helping them develop criteria of fairness and partnership. If we train them to think, speak, sell, and execute agreements that satisfy everyone, we will be equipping the leaders of tomorrow with negotiating skills proven to build and maintain empires with integrity.

Negotiate Like a Phoenician

We finalize with a quick synopsis. We presented a concept anyone can use anywhere, Tradeables™. Tradeables™ can come naturally in the course of DEAL methodology. In the acronym of DEAL the letter L stands for the leverage generated by Tradeables™.

We not only discussed the acronym, DEAL (D=Drivers, E=Entrapments, A=Analysis, L=Leverage, but we offered a review of the analysis tool of the 6 P's of negotiation (Person, Product, Problems, Process, Power, Prognosis; *see Appendix A*). Every negotiation can be broken into its parts to uncover bottlenecks and potential Tradeables™. Use of Tradeables™ suppresses moments of tension, easily capable of scuttling any DEAL.

As a prologue on *How to Produce Tradeables™*, the topic of Chapter IV:

- Follow all the steps to find the undisclosed needs of the other party.
- Know in advance what is within your reach to satisfy those discovered needs.
- Avoid promising Tradeables™. A promise unfulfilled gains no leverage, even if totally separate from the scope of the present negotiation.
- Be observant of your customer's conversations, office space, environment, and behaviors.
- Remember that Tradeables™ can be spontaneous or planned, such as coupons or stickers. They can be customized or from a template.
- Avoid confusing nibble tactics with Tradeables™. Nibble tactics are additional conditions on the DEAL which may make the DEAL more attractive.
- If Tradeables™ became industry standards, they lose leveraging power.

- Don't be afraid to ask.
- Look for opportunities to empathize using tools like mirroring, paraphrasing, and active listening to get beyond superficial conversations.
- Once beyond superficial conversation, Tradeables™ are more likely to be revealed as information exchange uncovers needs.
- Be yourself (assuming you are honest, trustworthy, respecting, etc). Otherwise, try to incorporate the practices of the Phoenicians and be amazed at the response.

What are Tradeables™? Tradeables™ are favors unexpected by the other side outside of a DEAL which set the tone for future business dealings. The side creating Tradeables™ doesn't expect any direct reciprocity from the party receiving the Tradeables™. Tradeables™ are by definition outside of the scope of the initial negotiation. Tradeables™ with conditions become Trade-ins or Trade-offs during the negotiation process. Gifts or favors with the intent to manipulate or buy an inside position are not Tradeables™. The spirit of Tradeables™ is one of elevating the other person and business concern above the present DEAL. The Phoenician business model is one of fairness, openness, and integrity. Use of Tradeables™ must be within that overall framework of building a business partnership with mutual gain and mutual trust.

Finally, we could not discuss Phoenician business without discussing their use of technology for leverage. It seems that there is a connection between technological savvy and the potential for business

TraDEAbLes™

profit. The Phoenicians were technologically advanced for their time and were both merchants and engineers according to literature. Does this mean that a good engineer is a good negotiator? Not necessarily; however, they have goals in common. A good engineer solves needs creatively, and a good negotiator creatively solves needs. Are you using technology to give your business a competitive advantage? Are you able to use technology to create new markets? Are there unused technologies that could help you better meet the needs of your clients?

Learn to Negotiate Like a Phoenician!

Phoenician silver didrachm
Owl with crook and flail, Tyre mint, c. 332-306 BCE
Courtesy of Joseph Sermarini, http://www.forumancientcoins.com

Epitaph on Roman tombstone:

I am what you will be

But we add …
So make a difference while you can!

Sources

Aburdene, P. *Megatrends 2010: The Rise of Conscious Capitalism.* Charlottesville, VA: Hampton Roads Publishing, 2005.

Albenda, Pauline. *The Palace of Sargon, King of Assyria: Monumental Wall Reliefs at Dur-Sharrukin, from Original Drawings Made at the Time of Their Discovery in 1843-1844 by Botta and Flandin.* Paris: Editions Recherche sur les civilizations, 1986.

Chamoun-Nicolás, Habib. *DEAL: Guidelines for a Flawless Negotiation.* 3rd Ed., Kingwood: Key Negotiations, 2004.

Godolphin, Francis (ed). *The Greek Historians: The Complete and Unabridged Historical Works of Herodotus, Thucydides, Xenophon, and Arrian.* Vol. 1-2. New York, NY: Random House, 1942.

Harden, Donald. *The Phoenicians.* New York, NY: Praeger, 1962.

Herm, Gerhard. *The Phoenicians.* Edited by Caroline Hillier. New York, NY: William Morrow and Company, 1975.

Herodotus. *The Histories.* Translated by George Rawlinson. New York, NY: Alfred A. Knopf, 1997.

Hoehner, Harold. *Herod Antipas: A Contemporary of Jesus Christ.* Grand Rapids, MI: Zondervan, 1980.

Holst, Sanford. *Phoenicians: Lebanon's Epic Heritage.* Los Angeles, CA: Cambridge & Boston Press, 2005.

Holy Bible, New International Version. Grand Rapids, MI: Zondervan, 1984.

Johnston, Thomas. *Did the Phoenicians Discover America?* Houston: St. Thomas Press, 1965.

Josephus. *The Life and Works of Flavius Josephus.* Translated by William Whiston. New York, NY: Holt, Rinehart and Winston, 1957.

Josephus. *The New Complete Works of Josephus.* Translated by William Whiston. Grand Rapids, MI: Kregel Publications, 1999.

Khalaf, Salim. *A Bequest Unearthed Phoenicia – Encyclopedia Phoeniciana.* (2006) Accessed on 12/20/2006, http://phoenicia.org.

Layard, A. H. Monuments of Nineveh. London: John Murray, 1853, pl. 31.

Markoe, Glenn. *Peoples of the Past, Phoenicians.* Berkeley, CA: University of California Press, 2000.

Matthiae, Paolo. *Geschichte der Kunst im Alten Orient.* Stuttgart: Theiss, 1999.

Moscati, Sabatina. *The World of the Phoenicians.* Edited by Alastair Hamilton. New York, NY: Praeger, 1968.

Moscati, Sabatina. *The Phoenicians.* New York, NY: Abbeville Press, 1988.

Secrets of Archaeology: Sailing with the Phoenicians. (DVD) Wheeling, IL: Film Ideas, 2003.

Toffler, A., and Toffler, H., *Revolutionary Wealth*, Alfred A. Knopf, 2006.

White, Sherwin. *The Letters of Pliny.* London: Oxford University Press, 1966.

Appendix A: Review of analysis methodology from *DEAL – Guidelines to a Flawless Negotiation*

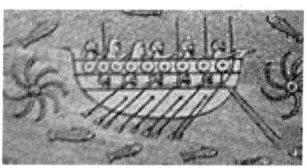

Phoenician vessels, Assyrian relief, Nineveh (after Layard, 1853)

Negotiation – A Strategy for Life

Negotiations are intrinsic to human nature and to our everyday life. At work, we negotiate with our peers, supervisors, and clients to effectively achieve the goals of our organization. We do the same with our spouses in order to satisfy our expectations and desire to build a positive and happy life together. With our children, we negotiate as part of the process of their upbringing. We even negotiate with ourselves when, for example, we are reconciling eating something for which we have an intense craving (like a food high in calories, fat and cholesterol) with the objectives of health and/or aesthetics, so important in our quality of life. To negotiate is definitely inherent to human nature.

Negotiating cross-culturally means searching for the understanding of people, their values, and the dynamics of their interactions (negotiations) at work, at home, at school, in self-reflection, and across all the vectors of the human process. Cross-cultural negotiations was a recurring theme in my book, *DEAL: Guidelines for a Flawless Negotiation.* Seeking deals outside our own culture simply requires more preparation and understanding. You have to know not only your negotiating strategy, but you must become familiar with client needs within the context of his culture. In this global society, you don't have to cross borders to need culturally sensitive negotiation skills.

In the prevailing business climate, we advocate the traditional salesman to become a business developer for his client. This global vision begins by focusing on the needs of the client and his overall business health. We are asked to think, "How do we develop our client's business? What can we offer him to make his business grow?" This leads us to promote robust and efficient negotiations. Robust negotiations are conducted in such a way that the client will call us again. Thus, we repeat the new business development circle. Robust negotiations lead us to develop relationships with our clients that are progressively stronger and longer term and require more of our attention, similar to a tree that grows and flourishes when well cared for. The more robust our relationship is with our clients, the more it will require constant cultivation. The relationship grows from a robust negotiation with the client and, as a result, so does the development of new business.

The 6 P's

As outlined in "**Deal**", a vision of global negotiation could be achieved by breaking down any negotiation into six fundamental elements.

People	the players
Process	the negotiation process and its parts
Power	the sources of power
Product	the element under negotiation or the business opportunity analyzed (*applicable also to services rendered or policy*)
Problem	the matter in dispute or conflict
Prognosis	the forecast element

People
The P of "People" or "Players" is the main focus of Dr. Chamoun's research and is the most important P of all. After all, we are negotiating with people all the time – people with different business habits and cultures. So if we can get a better understanding of their issues, business models, and habits, we are more likely to achieve better results when we negotiate with them. The book *DEAL* focuses on the different cultural aspects of the P of "People or "the players" and their affect on negotiation style. Culture is defined not only as the customs, institutions and achievements of a nation or people, but also as the corporate, professional, and personal communication behaviors and attitudes of people groups, including the role of gender.

TraDEAbLes™

Process
The "Process", or the negotiation process, is also discussed at depth in the literature. The act of negotiation is a time consuming effort. It is not a single directed activity without interrelation. Instead, it is a continuous process that needs to be understood fully by all the negotiating parties. Sometimes understanding is more important to the process than the substance we are negotiating. Negotiators, having the tendency to focus on substance, can easily forget the process and fail to obtain win/win negotiations. There are many known treatises that explain the science of negotiation and its complexities (*see suggested reading*, Breslin and Rubin, 1999; Nierenberg, 1995; Pruitt, 1991; Raiffa, 2000; Walton, 1965; Watkins, 2002; Young, 1994; Zartman 1991; Shell, 2006, Thompson, 2005, Pekar and Colson, 2004, etc.).

Power
The P of "Power" is the power of negotiation, and many authors have explained the sources of power and the importance of power over the negotiating parties and the outcome (*see suggested reading*, Cohen, 1982: Cohen, 2003; Stark, 1995; Karras, 1992; Hawkins, 1995).

Product
The "Product", is sometimes referred to as the business opportunity and can be an actual product, service, or policy. This 'P' has been carefully analyzed by many authors of sales methodologies. Most of the methodologies help the readers concentrate on analyzing the opportunity, the decision makers, the

influencers, and the decision-making process. They also help define the client's needs and wants. In summary, the methodologies help the sellers find out if there is a real opportunity, if he can compete, if he can win, and if it is worth the effort of pursuing the specific opportunity. These sales methodologies help the seller understand the buyer's vision of the decision-making process as he is buying.

Problem
When negotiating conflicts, the "Problem" is a completely different ball game and is referred to as the mediation process where a third party comes into play. There are numerous authors on conflict resolution and mediation (*see suggested reading*, Fisher,1989,1996; HBR, 2000; Pruitt 1986; Stone, Patton and Heen, 2000; Susskind and Field, 1996; Ury, 1991, 2000).

Prognosis
The ability to accurately forecast the outcome of the negotiation is a function of how much knowledge and understanding one has of the external factors that affect one's industry and market. The P of "Prognosis" reminds us of the uncertainties that could make deals turn sour.

DEAL is all about dissecting any negotiation into six pieces and analyzing each one at a time. We always need to assess which P is the most critical and write a strategy to precede the negotiation with different options and alternatives.

TraDEAbLes™

The 6 P's in Action

CASE STUDY A: Trust

The blank check extended to Phoenician King Hiram by King Solomon is the ultimate expression of a business relationship built on trust. We examine a real-life modern scenario where trust was essential to reaching a DEAL.

John, an American from the south, is visiting a Mexican potential customer, Pedro. Pedro is not a typical successful Mexican business man. Although it is not a good practice to create stereotypes, a typical successful Mexican business man is *all business* and *always on time*. Pedro, on the other hand, is a manager with unorthodox business practices, (i.e., *is always late* and *takes more business appointments than he can handle*). The only positive thing about Pedro is that once the supplier catches his attention, he pays a premium for the services. Then he is very generous and pays on time.

John on the other hand is not a flexible global business mindset type of person. He is a more old fashioned business man with a signature phrase of "my way or the highway."

John visits Mexico on a company "Consult" proposal discussion meeting with Pedro. This is John's first time international assignment. John is a very successful business developer for company "Consult" in the States, and most of John's customers' headquarters are in the USA. His ability to bring cash flow to company "Consult" was his asset. John's inexperience in dealing with international customers was obvious. John's attitudes of "know it all", "Company 'Consult' is the best in its class", and "I am the top salesman" didn't get him far with Pedro's appointment in Mexico.

During the breakfast meeting at a prestigious restaurant in Mexico City, John started talking "all business," and Pedro didn't listen at all. In fact, Pedro had to leave the table on several occasions to answer his cell phone and left John with Pedro's assistant Maria to take notes on John's proposal. If we step back for a minute, Pedro was trying to send a message to John by delegating the proposal to Maria. John didn't read it correctly. Instead, he continued presenting the proposal to Maria. At the end of the breakfast, John took a plane back to Atlanta with false high expectations of a deal.

Several months went by after John's visit to Mexico City, and no sales were made, nor were there any signs of Pedro or his assistant. In fact, company "Consult" business developer for international affairs, Drew, an international experienced Anglo Saxon, made a new appointment to meet Pedro in Mexico City.

Drew went to a breakfast meeting with Pedro and concentrated on understanding Pedro's needs; Drew spoke on more unrelated topics to the proposal than the actual proposal. Drew concentrated on developing a relationship with Pedro, and both developed an instant connection.

Drew came back from his Mexico trip with a sale that represented 40% of his sales quota for the year. You may wonder, what did Drew do that John didn't do? Both were Anglo Saxons and season experienced sales executives. Drew had to "break the equilibrium" or "status quo" and "generate harmony" with the other party, Pedro.

When dealing with different cultures, there are things that are negotiable, things that aren't negotiable, and things that don't need to be negotiated.
1) Business behavior and attitudes are negotiable.
2) Values and principles aren't negotiable.
3) Respect and tolerance are a given and don't need to be negotiated.

Breaking Drew's equilibrium or status quo from this case study was exemplified by going from an "all business attitude" to a "relationship building attitude" and being patient to talk business only when Pedro was ready to talk business. John, on the other hand, didn't feel at ease working outside his comfort zone and demonstrated "his way or the highway" attitude doesn't work in all business environments. John didn't know that international business has a mystique to it. Drew got the sale by being patient and understanding that a different context needs a different approach.

A successful international negotiator needs to be flexible, open, stereotype-free, and, most of all, patient and tolerant. We can capture in one word the international negotiator mind frame: TRUST. Let's analyze the word TRUST.

T The international negotiator needs to **T**ransport or **T**ranscend itself into the other culture, putting aside all his business behaviors and attitudes for a moment.

R **R**especting others is the basis of any healthy long term business relationship. So many times we hear parents tell their kids, "I'd rather have your **R**espect than your love." Although parents may not mean it, **R**espect is a priority.

U **U**nderstanding together with patience, humility, and acceptance of other business behaviors and attitudes is what negotiating internationally is all about.

S **S**tand for your own values and principles. Never compromise your own values for a business transaction. Negotiating with values is a whole new game. Be honest and honorable when dealing with different cultures. It is a rule of life; honesty goes a long way, especially for long term relationship building. Don't lose the honor for the business, because you will end up loosing the business and the honor.

T Last, but not of least importance, is **T**olerance. Be **T**olerant; remember that the key to success in a long term business relationship is **TRUST** (**T**ransport, **R**espect, **U**nderstanding, **S**tand, and **T**olerance).

TraDEAbLes™

CASE STUDY B: Determination

Just like the Phoenician woman who approached Jesus, sometimes the key to achieving your desired negotiation outcome is persistence.

To have a better understanding, let's walk through a case study where Jack is on his way to the airport to take a 7:00 p.m. flight from Mexico to Texas. Jack had one thing in his mind – get on the next available airplane, the 5:00 p.m. flight. Catching the earlier flight was a matter of "death or life," because Jack had a personal meeting at his church, a yearly celebration that he couldn't miss. However, because of an important business event and a flight delay, he was caught in this situation.

- Only the 5:00 p.m. flight will give him time to arrive at the celebration. Otherwise, he will miss the event.

- The day of the event was during peak vacation season. The chances that Jack would find an empty seat on the earlier plane were very slim.

- Jack arrives at the airport precisely at the time all the passengers from the 5:00 p.m. flight were checked in and waiting to pre-board the airplane.

Technically, he didn't have a chance, and it was too late to accept anyone even on a standby basis, according to the airline procedures and rules. Jack went through 12 "NO's" to obtain the "YES." Let's analyze how this happened. Upon arrival to the airport, Jack went to the airline ticketing counter and asked the attendant, Marilyn, if it were possible to change to the earlier plane. Marilyn replies, "No way, Sir. Even though the plane is still at the gate, and there is space on the plane, standard operational procedures say that no one else can board the airplane." Jack replies, "Could you please pass my request to your supervisor, because I need to be there? My wife is organizing a church event, and if I am not there, I am in trouble." She replies, "I understand, Sir. If I were in your situation, I would be in trouble too. Let me ask Mr. Thomas; however, I cannot assure you anything. Even if he said okay, it is doubtful you could make it to Gate 29 in time."

Mr. Thomas denied the request. He spoke to operations 5 minutes ago, and the number of passengers for this flight was already finalized. Mr. Thomas said, "If you were here 10 minutes ago, we might have been able to accommodate you. Please don't even bother to go to the gate because this flight is closed, the gate is far away, and you still must clear security. During this peak travel period, the lines are especially long."

To his disappointment, Jack, a negotiator by nature, didn't close this issue. He thanked Mr. Thomas and Marilyn for the efforts and wished them a Merry Christmas before taking off to Gate 29. Even though Jack received several negatives, he had an alternative to the non-agreement, his original flight. He passed the security inspection very quickly. For some reason, the line was moving faster than normal.

TraDEAbLes™

Upon approaching Gate 29, Jack heard a gentle voice beckoning over the speaker, "We will start pre-boarding flight X at Gate 29 shortly. All passengers please be in the vicinity of Gate 29."

Jack was very happy, and his hopes went up after hearing that the flight had not yet pre-boarded, although he was told that operations has closed the flight, and the computer indicated no more passengers were being accepted. Jack finally arrived at Gate 29 and greeted the gate attendant with a big smile and renewed courage. After catching his breath from the long walk, he reads the name tag of the attendant, Vicky. He said, "Vicky, could you help me?"

Vicky replied, "Certainly, that will be my pleasure, Sir."

Jack knew then that Vicky had a great attitude and a courteous and polite disposition. He thought to himself, "This is it, I am going on this plane." Jack petitions Vicky, "Could you please check into the possibility of me catching this plane, because my wife is organizing a church event, and I need to be present, or I could be in trouble.

Vicky replies, "Oh, you are not on this flight? You must be on the later flight. That is nice, thinking about your wife. Let me see what I can do for you. Well... There is space on this plane. Would you like an aisle or window seat?"

Jack replied, "An aisle seat would be great. Thanks a lot, I really appreciate it."

Vicky said, "Okay, let me change your reservation, and we will be boarding shortly." When Vicky was making the change, the computer didn't allow her to add Jack. She came back to Jack saying, "I am really sorry, but the computer is not allowing me to assign your seat. I'm afraid you will have to keep your original flight. I am really sorry. I did everything I could."

Jack replied, "Oh no!"

Vicky called the check in desk manager Mr. Thomas, and Vicky said, "There is a fine man that is trying to get on this plane. I tried to change his ticket, but the computer is not allowing it. I need to change his ticket back to the original flight, could you help?"

Mr. Thomas said, "Yes, he was here, and I told him there is no way he can go on this flight."

Vicky tells Jack what Mr. Thomas said. Jack replied, "Yes, I understood also that I probably wouldn't make it to the gate in time, but since I am here, and you have not even pre-boarded, I wanted to try anyway."

Vicky gives Jack his ticket back and said, "Well, Sir, here is your ticket for the next flight. Sorry again, have a great evening".

Before Jack wanders away, Mr. Thomas calls Vicky mentioning that he called operations, and it was OK to let Jack board this plane.

What is the moral of the story? After analyzing the six P's of *DEAL* methodology, we find the following: The biggest issue was the P of Process. That was the bottleneck in the negotiation. That was a closed issue for all of the airline attendants, except for the gate agent Vicky until the computer didn't allow her to give a seat that was physically available. The P of Person was not an issue. Everyone had a great attitude and was willing to help solve a passenger problem. The passenger was a nice person, not a difficult conflictive type. Although Marilyn and Mr. Thomas were closed on the Process issue, they were open on the People issue and willing to build a relationship with their customer, Jack. While Mr. Thomas was closed at the beginning, he did change at the very end from closed to open. Perhaps he thought, "Well, he (Jack) is already there at the gate, they haven't start boarding, and he hasn't any checked luggage." Maybe Mr. Thomas and Marilyn discussed the issue and felt they could do something for this passenger that really needed to go on this plane. Thus, it was worth it to talk to Operations and request a possible status change which would allow the passenger to board. Jack built rapport with all of the decision makers and influencers (Mr. Thomas, Marilyn, and Vicky). They had nothing to lose by trying one last call to Operations.

This was not a fabrication but a true anecdote where relationship building and a positive attitude established the right conditions for a WIN-WIN outcome. This is possible in every life and business activity if we stop and analyze our issues in terms of the six P's: Process, Person, Prognosis, Problem, Power, and Product.

In this case, the P of Process transitioned from open-closed to open-open with different decision makers. Remember going from closed-open to open-open requires considerable effort and energy. Never give up if the final objective is worth it. We need to evaluate if it is worth the effort. Sometimes it's not. Sometimes it is. In summary,

- Be persistent
- Know the Process and the Players (People)
- Judge your demands objectively
- Take a chance
- A "NO" could be a hidden "YES"
- If it is worth it, NEVER GIVE UP

The following checklist exercise concerning one of your own current or past negotiation experiences will help you become familiar with the 6 P's.

Never, never, never give up! – **Winston Churchill.**

TraDEAbLes™

6 P's Analysis Checklist

SIX P's Negotiation Checklist according to CHAMOUN©2004

1. PERSON (Decision Makers Analysis)

Before checking the statements below, think about a negotiation you are about to undertake, you have executed or you are in the middle of. If you agree with the following statements mark an x inside the parentheses shown below. If you don't agree, leave it blank:

1. Chemistry exists with your counterpart ☐
2. It is fairly easy to break the ice ☐
3. Your counterpart doesn't use negotiation hardball tactics ☐
4. I have an idea of the counterpart's strengths and weaknesses ☐
5. The counterpart is not indirect ☐
6. The counterpart doesn't evade you or your peers ☐
7. The counterpart is not a difficult person to deal with ☐
8. The counterpart is a relationship builder ☐
9. You are not intimidated by the counterpart ☐
10. The counterpart is an objective person ☐

RESULT (PERSON) (Add up all the above marked statements) ____
Each mark counts as a point
PERSON represents a % bottleneck = (10-RESULT)* 10 = % Person ____

189

2. PROBLEM (Negotiation Context Analysis)

1. There is no history with this negotiation (no experience) ☐
2. This negotiation is not the renegotiation of an existing project ☐
3. This is a simple negotiation without any complexity ☐
4. There is no conflict among the parties ☐
5. The matter to be negotiated is not conflictive ☐
6. The matter to be negotiated is not a matter of "life or death" ☐
7. It doesn't include any preconceived idea or negative predisposition against any of the parties ☐
8. No hard feelings or apathy among the parties is present ☐
9. This negotiation is the product of an error or contingency ☐
10. Scope of work promised has not been delivered by any of the parties ☐

RESULT (PROBLEM) (Add up all the above marked statements) _____
Each mark counts as a point
PROBLEM is a % bottleneck = (10-RESULT)* 10 = **% Problem** _____

3. PROCESS (Negotiation Sequence Analysis)

1. This negotiation doesn't require several visits to different decision makers ☐
2. There is no sequence to negotiation ☐
3. Paperwork is not an issue to start negotiation ☐
4. The negotiation process is not long and tedious ☐
5. Buying process doesn't go by several decision makers ☐
6. Payment process doesn't go through several decision makers ☐

TraDEAbLes™

7. You know and understand the steps of the buying process ☐
8. You know and understand the steps of the purchasing process ☐
9. You know all the decision makers of the buying process ☐
10. You know all the decision makers of the purchasing process ☐

RESULT (PROCESS) (Add up all the above marked statements) ____
Each mark counts as a point
PROCESS is a % bottleneck = (10-RESULT)* 10 = **% Process** ____

4
PRODUCT (Negotiated Subject Analysis)

1. Your product has unique characteristics in the market place ☐
2. There are no substitute products for yours ☐
3. You are delivering the product that you promised ☐
4. You know the benefits your counterpart is getting from your product ☐
5. Your product is innovative, and your client is convinced of it ☐
6. Your product "will cure your client's pain" and not just be a "temporary pain reliever" ☐
7. Your product is not a "commodity" only competing by price ☐
8. Your counterpart will have a great negative impact on critical business issues by not acquiring your product ☐
9. You know your product's advantages and disadvantages in comparison with your competitors from your counterpart's point of view ☐
10. Your product has value added over your competitors ☐

RESULT (PRODUCT) (Add up all the above marked statements) ____
Each mark counts as a point
PRODUCT is a % bottleneck = (10-RESULT)* 10 = **% Product** ____

191

5 PROGNOSIS (Analysis of alternatives)

1. You have a "Plan B" ☐
2. You know your best alternative to the negotiated agreement ☐
3. You know your counterpart's best alternative to the negotiated agreement ☐
4. You are aware of your worst alternative if you don't reach agreement ☐
5. You are aware of your counterpart's worst alternative if you don't reach agreement ☐
6. You have considered options to the agreement, and you have it in writing ☐
7. You have an escape plan to get away from the deal ☐
8. You have a landing plan to close the deal ☐
9. You have strategies in writing for the worst, best, and normal scenarios ☐
10. You have evaluated what will happen to the relationship if you don't reach agreement ☐

RESULT (PROGNOSIS) (Add up all the above marked statements) ____
Each mark counts as a point
PROGNOSIS is a % bottleneck = (10-RESULT)* 10 = % Prognosis ____

TraDEAbLes™

6 POWER (perceived power analysis)

1. Your counterpart is not a monopoly ☐
2. There is a coalition among suppliers to the point that negotiation power is high ☐
3. Your product is not a "commodity" ☐
4. Your product is very competitive ☐
5. There is no threat of substitute products or new market entries ☐
6. It is not feasible for the buyers of your products to form alliances ☐
7. You have a niche market product, high markup, or high profitability ☐
8. Your counterpart and their offices & products don't intimidate you ☐
9. You have prepared on all the negotiation aspects ☐
10. You are not afraid of making a fool out of yourself by asking ☐

RESULT (POWER) (Add up all the above marked statements) ___
Each mark counts as a point
POWER represents a % bottleneck = (10-RESULT)* 10 = **% Power** ___

A man needs a good mirror to scrutinize his heart as well as his face.

Plautus, Epidicus

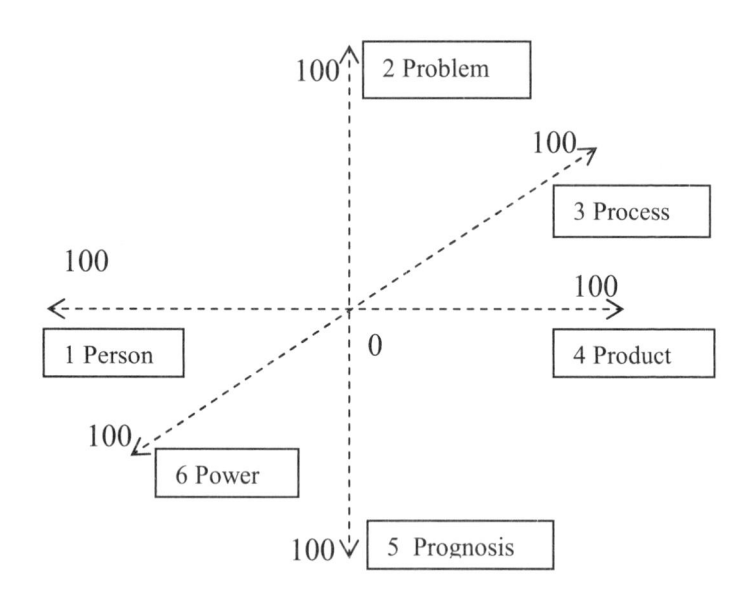

```
         100↑  | 2 Problem |
                      100↘
                         | 3 Process |
100                      100
←---------------|---------------→
| 1 Person |    0        | 4 Product |
  100↙
     | 6 Power |
          100↓ | 5 Prognosis |
```

Plot each P (%) on the appropriate axis

The resulting percentages (%) are plotted on the corresponding axes (Person, Problem, Process, Product, Prognosis, and Power), forming a spider plot. The highest point depicts the negotiation bottleneck at a given point in time. As a matter of illustration, let's say that Prognosis is equal to 70%, and every other P is equal to 30%. This means that we need to work on a Plan B for the negotiation being analyzed.

TraDEAbLes™

Appendix B: Short Stories and Articles

Stories make concepts real. Through stories and role-play, we can relate to our own situation, study and understand our actions, and project and predict our future interactions.

This first article has the intention to take the reader by the hand through the 6 P's of negotiation analysis introduced in Chapter I. The idea is to read and follow the 6 P's analysis to generate a vision. The vision of the negotiation using the 6 P's is to find which P is closed and how to open it. Depending on the analysis result, we can open a closed P, meaning finding and addressing the bottleneck to reaching an agreement.

1. Negotiating when you are CLOSED and the other is OPEN

When faced with an impasse in a negotiation, first, we have to ask ourselves which of the 6 P's is CLOSED (Person, Product, Problem, Process, Power, and Prognosis). In this context, CLOSED means the way to making a DEAL is blocked. Likewise, the term OPEN is used to signify no obstacle to moving forward. If we have a CLOSED portion of the process, we must find out why it is CLOSED. Is it a lack of communication?

Is it a misunderstanding? Is it a rule or procedure that is not allowing us to OPEN? Is it an attitude or behavioral problem that is causing the CLOSED? Is it an ego situation? Is there a sequence that we must follow before we can OPEN any CLOSED issues? Is it a lack of knowledge? Is this a negotiation with negative energy people? Etc. Next, we must probe how negotiable is the P which is CLOSED?

Before entering a negotiation we need to know:

1) What is negotiable?
2) What is not?
3) What issues don't need to be negotiated?

For every P that is CLOSED, if it is not negotiable, or if something doesn't need to be negotiated, simply move on. Don't waste your time and the time of others trying to negotiate something that is not negotiable or already has been negotiated. Focus on what is possible to be negotiated.

It is easier to negotiate attitudes and behavior over values, norms, and laws. So, find out if the CLOSED issue is a value, behavior, or attitude. Before planning your negotiation strategy, find out the degree of difficulty and possible energy consumption on OPENING the CLOSED issue. Is it worth it or not? Is there a relationship or not?

Finally, we need to plan a negotiation strategy to OPEN the CLOSED issue. It takes considerably more effort to OPEN a CLOSED issue for the other party.

The negotiation strategy elements are: Energy, Timing, Decision makers, and Sequence. Our negotiation energy is not created or destroyed, only transformed and possibly stored. So, let's keep our negotiation energy until the right time to OPEN the CLOSED issues with the proper sequence and decision makers.

Let's examine the case of John's SUV lease renegotiation.

One fine day, John took his SUV to the dealership for maintenance service. While waiting in the dealership lobby, he had a wish to turn in the old SUV and get a brand new one. It was a wish, because he didn't want to increase his monthly lease payment. Also, he didn't want to pay any penalty for early termination of his present lease contract or condition of the vehicle.

He decided to talk to the salesperson, Roger, and find out if it was feasible. So he inquired, "Dear Roger could you help me? I want to know if I can turn in my old SUV for a new one. I am not interested in paying more than my present monthly lease, nor am I interested in paying any down payment or penalty. Practically, I just want to turn in the old deal and get out of the dealership today with a new SUV and the current monthly payment. Could you find out if it is feasible?"

Roger replied, "John, what model SUV and color do you want?"

John responded, "The same as mine. It is an LXU, and we don't care about the color. Which ones are available?"

Roger went back to his office to inspect the year-end inventory, because new vehicles were coming in. He found five different choices. Finally, John picked out a gray one.

"Okay, John, do you mind if we check your credit history, so we can give you the monthly conditions?"

John said, "Go right ahead. Just remember I am paying $ 432 /month and don't want to change my leasing plan conditions. I just want the same lease conditions as before: a 3-year lease contract and 15,000 miles per year."

Actual situation: John has a 3-year contract to lease a Utility Vehicle for $432 /month on a 15,000 miles/yr basis. John's lease expires in 15 months, and he has already gone over the 2 year mileage mark (31,000 miles). The existing conditions were as follows:

1) The windshield was hit by a small rock, and it has a small fracture less than a dollar bill, which is apparent from the front. This will most likely grow with the changes in the weather.
2) The tires haven't been changed, and it is recommended doing so at 31,000 miles.
3) The SUV inspection sticker is due a couple of months from now.
4) Licenses plates are also expiring in a month.

5) The next lease payment is due a month from today.
6) The value of the SUV is $20,000, including an upgrade with a VHS system.
7) John owes, as of today, $21,450.

This case happens at the end of summer season when the new models are coming in. The salesmen at the dealership need to get rid of all the old models. The decision makers at the dealership are the financial officer and the salesman. The salesman's motivation was the sales commission, and the financial officer's motivations were to position new leases and allocate more debt. Mrs. Summers, financial officer of the dealership, was willing to waive the amount due on the old lease of $1450.

Roger comes back to John with 4 options as follows.

Option 1:	Option 2:
15,000 miles / 36 month lease $505-$515 monthly	12,000 miles /36 month lease $480 - $490 monthly
Option 3:	Option 4:
15,000 miles / 48 month lease $465- $475 monthly	12,000 miles / 48 month lease $440 - $450 monthly

The range of lease per month is a function of John's credit rating. If he had a great credit history, then he will be paying the lower end of the range.

John had already expressed his ideal negotiation outcome, which was Option 1, but without paying anything extra. However, this option's lease range was outside John's expectations and aspirations ($505-$515). John said, "Well, I guess I didn't make myself clear. I don't want to pay anything more than I am paying today. Could you call the finance officer to see if there is anything he can do?"

Roger responded, "Certainly, let me call Mrs. Summers, and I hope you realize that we are already waiving an amount due on the old lease of $1450.

Fifteen minutes pass by, and Mrs. Summers arrives. She greeted John saying, "I understand you want a new SUV. We have worked the numbers to make sure you are satisfied. We'll make an adjustment, and you will be paying the same amount $432 but with 12,000 miles per year (Option 2)."

John countered, "Mrs. Summers, I have two alternatives. One is to do nothing, park my SUV until I catch up with the miles, and turn it in at the end of the lease. After all, I will be traveling frequently by plane next year and won't need it much. This alternative will allow me to buy a luxury vehicle from a different dealership than yours, and you will lose a customer. The second alternative is to lease the new SUV at $432 per month with the terms of Option 1 (CLOSED-

TraDEAbLes™

OPEN). In this case, you get another three years of lease and could sell or lease my old SUV. The choice of alternatives is in your hand."

Mrs. Summers said, "Let me talk to my supervisor and see what we could do for you, especially since you are a long term customer at this dealership."

Mrs. Summers returned with a final offer. "Well, John, here is the deal. You will get Option 1 and pay only $450 / month. This is as good as it gets."

John replied, "Well, Mrs. Summers, thank you for your effort. I need to leave now."

Mrs. Summers responds, "I can't do anything else. We tried our best."

As John is getting up out of the chair to leave the office, he said to Mrs. Summer, "Split the difference, and you have a DEAL."

She replied, "Give me a minute." She came back and said, "Deal."

John smiled and said, "Okay, even though is not exactly what I had in mind, I accept. Could you at least give me some free oil change coupons?"

Mrs. Summers turned to Roger and asked, "Can you swing that?"

Roger gladly responded, "Sure! Anything for a loyal customer."

Roger told John, "My hat's off to you. I have observed the way you negotiated this deal, and I have never seen anyone like you. First you were very low key, obtaining all the data, and you were prepared. Then, when you knew everything and invested the time, you didn't lose control. Your energy level was always subdued. At the right moment of the negotiation, you came down like an avalanche of power, to the point that we felt we would lose the negotiation. Then, you made a DEAL for everyone: me, the finance manager, the dealership, and, most importantly, yourself."

What happened in this negotiation? John didn't have anything to lose and a lot to win. The Dealership has a lot to lose if John walked empty handed from the deal. For the sake of simplicity, let's consider two alternatives that John had.

Alternative 1: John may wait until the lease expired and buy or lease a new car from a different or the same dealership. (CLOSED-OPEN)

Alternative 2: John trades in the old lease for a new lease, and the dealer captivates another three-year lease.

The total lease amount that John has paid to the dealership for 1 year and 9 months has already been a profitable business for the dealership.

The dealership alternatives were:

Alternative 1: Trade in the old lease for the new one, and sell or refinance the old lease to a third party.

Alternative 2: Wait until the lease expiration date and consummate or turn in the old lease.

The lessons learned in this negotiation are:

1) Know the P of Person you are negotiating with and their critical issues.

2) Don't let the P of Process control you. Control the process.

John had a CLOSED-OPEN issue with the monthly lease and the leasing conditions. If he had OPEN-OPEN issues with either one, the negotiation time would have been shortened and other options would have satisfied the OPEN-OPEN demands.

OPEN-CLOSED issues to Mrs. Summers were to give the same conditions as an old lease to a new one. Roger had OPEN-OPEN issues because he had a positive attitude and wanted to sell the unit.

This negotiation was a success because everyone had some OPEN issues, including everyone's positive attitude. The relationship building was a key to success in this negotiation.

John had negative experiences at other dealerships (CLOSED-CLOSED) where the sales or finance managers had an attitude. John has proven that negotiator attitude has a great effect on the negotiation outcome. If negotiator attitude is filled with negative energy, this leads to an impasse in the negotiation in most cases.

What about Tradeables™? Were there any? Roger gave John his requested oil change coupons after the deal was affirmed; thus, the gift was external to this DEAL. Did the fact that John asked for the freebie invalidate the gift of coupons as Tradeables™? Probably not, rather the question posed related a previously unexposed customer need, which the salesman was happy to fulfill. Besides, when John returned for an oil change, he might just require additional services outside of his contract.

Negotiator Attitude shapes the form of the negotiation outcome.

We give of ourselves when we give the gift of words: encouragement, inspiration, guidance.

Wilferd A. Peterson

2. Negotiation and Technology

Phoenicians were celebrated as learned scribes, who passed on the modern alphabet, skilled seafarers and explorers, and gifted artisans and engineers according to Glenn Markoe in his book *Peoples of the Past, Phoenicians*. History records their ability to employ advanced shipbuilding technology and manufacturing expertise in glass and metallurgy for end-use products. Is there a relationship between good negotiators and good skillful analytical minds? While there does not seem to be a direct correlation in the data, technology can improve our negotiation capacity. This article is about modern technology and its effect on both teaching and conducting negotiations.

Teaching Negotiation at Corporations and Universities Using Technology Leads to Innovative and Effective Learning

Dr. Habib Chamoun-Nicolás, Keynegotiations

Presented on November 14 – 15, 2005 at the international conference on *New Trends in Negotiation Teaching: Toward a Trans-Atlantic Network*, PON-IRENE ESSEC Business School – Cergy, France

ABSTRACT

This article summarizes lessons learned from the use of technology in both teaching negotiation skills and conducting actual negotiations. Four different mixed-mode combinations of learning were implemented in workshops on negotiation over a three-year period. Technology strengths and weakness were evaluated by observation and informal interviews. Of particular interest was the role of culture in choice or effectiveness of technology. Several hypotheses for future validation are suggested dealing with the role of technology in teaching, the role of technology in reducing methodology to practice, and their inter-dependency.

TraDEAbLes™

Key observations in the use of technology were noted in both teaching negotiation and conducting real negotiations. In both instances, technology creates a safe place to either learn or negotiate. Exchanges using technology are filtered of emotion in both teaching and practice. Asynchronous methods allow for additional preparation and better responses, as they can help avoid reacting behaviors. In teaching, technology can both foster teamwork and promote participant commitment. In conducting negotiations, technology can aid in the separation of people and the problem, as well as reducing the time needed to find the real interests behind positions.

In cross-cultural negotiations, technology has the potential to dissolve cultural barriers, diffuse power tactics, and eliminate cultural taboos. Those with indirect negotiation styles can become more direct using technology. Negotiations with technology become more objective-oriented and generally lead to higher rates of closing than with face-to-face meetings.

Teaching negotiation using technology can be cost effective and efficient, but it demands, increased preparation, coordination, and infrastructure investment. Using technology interjects its own culture above and beyond the participant's own culture. Teaching negotiation should recognize and adapt to cultural influence in both the method of teaching and on what works in practice for a particular culture.

BACKGROUND

A New Business Climate

New global scenarios, including
- a) information and cybernetic revolution,
- b) new technological developments,
- c) global markets,
- d) decision making complexity,
- e) corporation organizations complexities,
- f) new technological production processes,
- g) communication and globalization,
- h) continuing growth requirements,
- i) global scale production and organization, and
- j) financial markets with sustained growth,

are driving forces for the use of technology in education as an effective and productive way of learning. According to WR Hambrecht, the retention rate in a face-to-face workshop is only 58% after 33 minutes and drops to a mere 15% after three weeks. Thus, the traditional single in-person teaching experience does not work very well from the learner and employer perspective. Since technology exists in the marketplace and will only accelerate in acceptance as standard business practice, it makes sense to incorporate technology to deliver and reinforce instructional material on negotiating.

Research indicates that multi-mode learning can boost the efficacy of the teaching-learning process. The hierarchy of learning modes, as seen in Figure 1, suggests active methods with a constructivist focus are preferable. Some of these modes can clearly use technology in the transference of ideas, norms, and methods.

What is E-learning technology?

E- learning is an acronym for Virtual Education, which is:

- Flexible,
- Open,
- Interactive, and
- Uses all the technological resources from Internet.

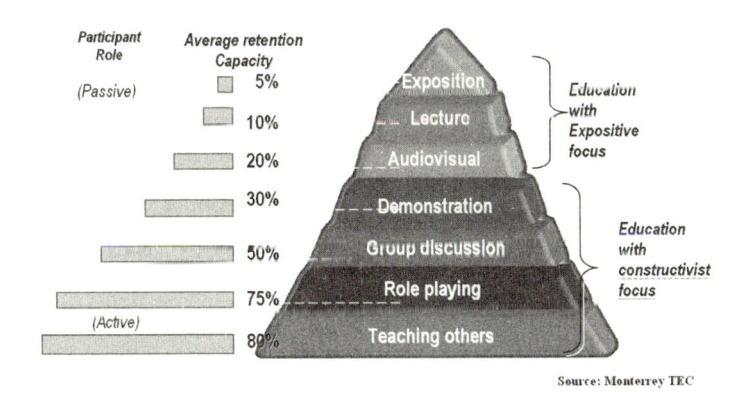

Fig. 1. Participant role and retention capacity for different modes of teaching.

E-learning involves teaching using internet technology and can assume many forms as delivered by network capability and internet standards. Some of the advantages of E-learning are:

- Access to a higher number of participants,
- Standardizes training,
- Facilitates training follow-up and evaluation,
- Promotes new learning techniques and better communication networks in participant's organization,
- Increases competitiveness through rapid adaptation and dissemination of new market demands, and
- Student participation is increased.

Using technology to teach negotiation requires a shift in the educational model from a professor-centered learning model to a participant-centered one. The participant has many resources at his disposal: tutors, digital libraries, study groups, self-paced modules, learning objectives, and the professor. In the particular case of negotiation, we use a didactic model for collaborative learning through problem-based learning (PBL), case studies, and project-based learning (PBL).

Course delivery using technology is a nested process of participant interaction with instructors and other learning resources with access to technological resources through a technology platform or infrastructure. It involves behind-the-scenes support and services provided by the teaching institution, such as administrative help, other faculty resources, and information technology support personnel. It can also involve infrastructure expected by the participant, such as an internet service provider. The interplay between these people and services in the use of technology in teaching is seen in Fig. 2.

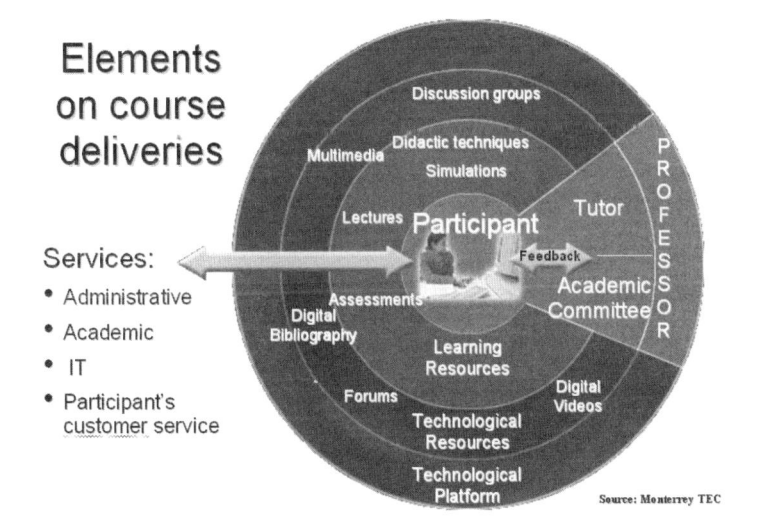

Fig. 2. Elements on course delivery in a participant-centered learning model.

Monterrey Institute of Technology has invested heavily in infrastructure for a virtual learning environment which spans the Americas. Their commitment to the use of technology in teaching is evidenced by the more than 100,000 students serviced in 2004 in its post-graduate, professional studies, continuous education, and social programs. Conducting workshops on negotiation is a portion of the Virtual University. Teaching negotiation using the internet has certain advantages. The internet:

- Helps present negotiation content on different levels,
- Offers several possibilities to widen participant's learning horizons (links, data bases, etc),
- Takes advantage of graphical and visual technology resources to enhance negotiation concept learning,
- Uses the technology of on-demand video,
- Promotes organized collaboration,
- Facilitates the use of diverse didactical techniques,
- Allows participants to develop search skills and conduct information analysis,
- Develops written communication skills and critical thinking,
- Allows evaluation of skills, attitudes, and knowledge, and
- Facilitates organization prior to the learning process.

Teaching negotiation using technology can be:

- Impersonal,
- Less centered on relationship building, and
- Impractical without proper technology infrastructure.

Further examination of the various technologies reveals the strengths and weaknesses outlined in Table 1.

METHODOLOGY

Teaching Modes

Six workshops were conducted over a three-year period with a focus on mixed modes of learning. These included face-to-face workshops, as well as and virtual synchronic and asynchrony methods. The different teaching modes used are as follows:

Method 1: Satellite transmission to more than thirty Monterrey TEC sites simultaneously of a live face-to-face negotiation workshop, followed by a debriefing session,

Method 2: Internet negotiation video presentation with multiple participants, followed by an online Q/A chat session, and

Method 3: Videoconference prior to the workshop, followed by a face-to-face workshop and a debriefing session by videoconference,

Method 4: A two-day, face-to-face, customized negotiation workshop, followed by virtual coaching sessions by the instructor for participants.

These methods are illustrated in Fig. 3a-d.

OBSERVATIONS

Some of the differences observed in teaching using technology over traditional face-to-face workshops are outlined in Table 2. In contrast, observations specific to using technology in negotiations within the Mexican culture are noted in Table 3. The role of technology in teaching and conducting negotiations is contrasted in Table 4. Some additional observations on conducting cross-cultural negotiations using technology include:

- Technology can dissolve cultural negotiation barriers.
- The client with whom you interact via technology may negotiate differently in person.
- One must assess when relationship is more important than convenience offered by technology, i.e. know your client.
- Negotiation using technology can potentially eliminate cultural taboos.
- Cultural power tactics can be diffused using technology.

Table 1. Strengths and weaknesses of various technologies for teaching negotiation

	Phone	Email	Chat	On-Demand Video	Video-Conferencing	Satellite Transmission
Global Reliability	👎	👍	👍	👍	👎	👎
Global Work Schedules	👎	👍	👍	👍	👎	👎
Personal Relationship Building	👍	👎	👍	👎	👍	👎
Infrastructure	👍	👍	👍	👍	👎	👎
Efficiency	👎	👍	👍	👍	👍	👍
Clarity	👎	👎	👎	👍	👍	👍
Immediacy	👍	👎	👍	👍	👍	👍
Filters Emotions	👎	👍	👍	👍	👎	👎
Expeditious	👍	👎	👍	👎	👎	👍
Overcoming Foreign Language Barriers	👎	👍	👍	👎	👎	👎

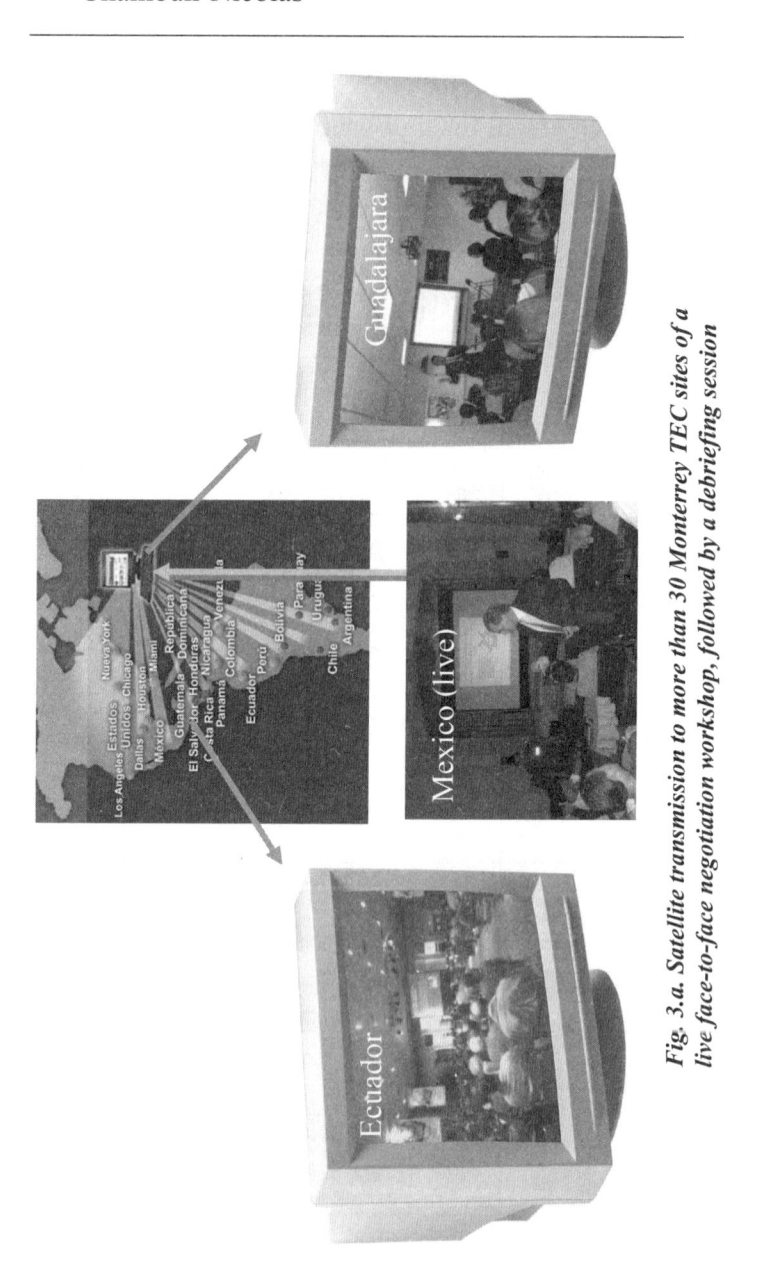

Fig. 3.a. Satellite transmission to more than 30 Monterrey TEC sites of a live face-to-face negotiation workshop, followed by a debriefing session

TraDEAbLes™

Guidelines for a flawless negotiation

Instructor: **Habib Chamoun-Nicolas**, Consultant

Topic: Negotiation
Duration: 2 hours

Summary:

It is proven that a "myopia" focusing on price only is generally the source of failure in negotiating; a global vision on the contrary provides successful situations for any corporation.

This conference will present a methodology to obtain the global vision of negotiation.
http://www.circulotec.com/servicios/videoteca/conferecistas/habib.htm

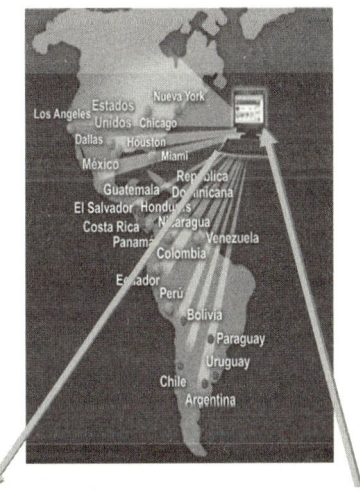

Fig. 3.b. Online video followed by Q/A Chat

Fig. 3.c. Video conference prior to a face-to-face workshop

217

Colombia face-to-face traditional

COACHING VIRTUAL

Negotiation Skills™

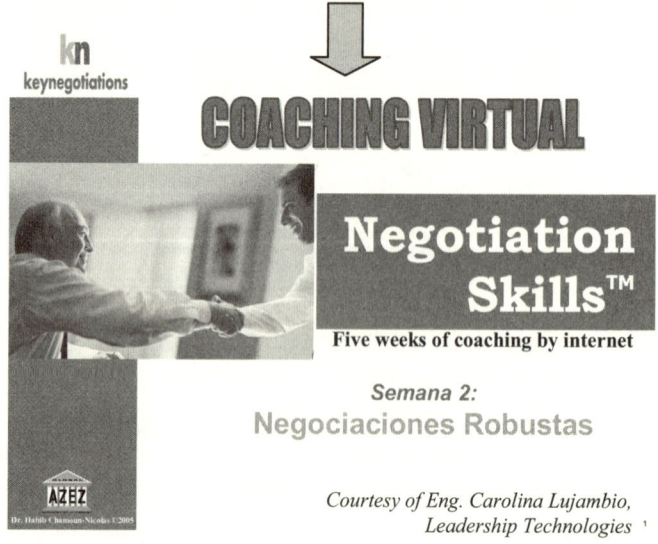

Five weeks of coaching by internet

Semana 2:
Negociaciones Robustas

Courtesy of Eng. Carolina Lujambio,
Leadership Technologies

Fig 3.d. A two day, face to face customized negotiation workshop, followed by virtual coaching

Table 2. Observations on the use of technology to teach negotiation.

Face-to-Face Workshop	Using Technology
More regionalized teaching	Wide dissemination; we transmitted simultaneously to more than 30 remote sites
Cases were only exposed to participants experiencing the workshop in person	Can show real cases in action
Cost per participant can be significant	Participants from multiple locations could comment and observe role-play negotiations
Participant travel often necessary	Forces written commitment
	Forces participants to define scope of work in black and white

Table 3. Observations on use of technology in negotiation within Mexican culture.

Face-to-Face Workshop	Using Technology
Relationship-oriented	More direct and impersonal
Emotionally-driven negotiation	Filter emotions
Hidden real interests behind the position	Can find real interest more quickly
Mexican Standoff	Objective-oriented negotiation
"Yes" means "No"	Rate of closing is higher
Lack of commitment	
No teamwork environment	

Table 4. Contrasting the role of technology in teaching negotiation skills versus conduction negotiations.

Teaching Negotiation	Conducting Negotiations
Creates a safe place to learn	Creates a safe place to negotiate
Helps filter emotions	Helps filter emotions
Asynchrony vs. synchronic (time to better prepare and avoid reacting)	Asynchrony vs. synchronic (time to better prepare and avoid reacting)
Fosters teamwork	Promotes People and Problem separation
Promotes participant commitment	Aids to find real interest behind positions
Broadens the learning experience	Homogenizes cultural differences

OPPORTUNITIES

There are a number of perceived trends, hypotheses, and open questions for scientific testing involving the use of technology in both teaching and conducting negotiations. While there are merits to the use of each technology implemented, it remains to be shown which technology or technologies in tandem will be the most efficient for learning. Alternatively, it remains to be seen what teaching modes are most effective for application of principles taught. This also leaves open the possibility that the teaching mode selected should be a function of the material taught.

With the increasing use of technology to conduct business locally and globally, should teaching materials and methods incorporate the technology tools to be applied in practice? Should teaching technology use be incorporated into teaching methods and materials? Since technology brings its own cultural imprint, perhaps teaching how to leverage negotiations using technology may be a fruitful avenue for instructors. This last point presumes that the best practice for technology use in negotiation is a mature subject, which is probably not the case.

SUMMARY

Mixed-mode learning is essential; E-learning tools can help meet this need. Teaching negotiation using technology can be cost-effective and efficient, but it demands increased preparation, coordination, and infrastructure investment.

Teaching negotiation should recognize and adapt to cultural influence in both the method of teaching and on what works in practice for a particular culture. However, using technology interjects its own culture, which can create some interesting synergies.

Key observations in the use of technology were noted in both teaching negotiation and conducting real negotiations. In both instances, technology creates a safe place to either learn or negotiate. Exchanges using technology are filtered of emotion in both teaching and practice. Asynchronous methods allow for additional preparation and better responses, as they can help avoid reacting behaviors. In teaching, technology can both foster teamwork and promote participant commitment. In conducting negotiations, technology can aid in the separation of people and the problem, as well as reducing the time needed to find the real interests behind positions.

In cross-cultural negotiations, technology has the potential to dissolve cultural barriers, diffuse power tactics, and eliminate cultural taboos. Those with indirect negotiation styles can become more direct using technology. Negotiations with technology become more objective-oriented and generally lead to higher rates of closing than with face-to-face meetings.

Learning new negotiations skills is a must when using technology to negotiate; thus, an opportunity exists to refine skill sets to better use technology tools to obtain win-win negotiation outcomes.

Wealth is above all an accumulation of possibilities

Gabriel Zaid

Suggested Reading

Adler, B., *How to Negotiate Like a Child*, Amacom, 2006.
Ávila, F., *Tácticas para la Negociación Internacional*, Trillas, 2000.
Axelrod, R., *The Evolution of Cooperation*, Basic Books, Inc. Publishers, 1984.
Bello, A., *The Sword and the Spirit*, Market Smart, 2005.
Blazquez, J.M, Alvar, J, and Wagner, C. *Fenicios y Cartagineses en el Mediterráneo*, Cátedra, 1999.
Brandenburger, A.M. and Nalebuff, B. J., *Co-opetition*. Currency Doubleday, 1998.
Breslin, W. and Rubin. J. W., *Negotiation Theory and Practice*, Program on Negotiation Books, 1999.
Breslin, W., "Breaking Away from Subtle Biases", *Negotiation Journal*, 5 (3), 1989, 219-222.
Casab, U., *Líbano desde Fenicia*, Academia Metropolitana, 2006.
Casse, P., *Training for Multicultural Manager: A Practical and Cross-cultural Approach to the Management of People*, Washington, D.C., SIERTAR International, 1982.
Chamoun-Nicolás, H., *Desarrollo de Negocios*, Agata, 2002.
Chamoun-Nicolás, H., "Aprenda a Cerrar Buenos Tratos", *Entrepreneur*, (Julio) 2002.
Chamoun-Nicolás, H., "*Trato Hecho-guía para una Negociación sin Fallas*", KN, 2003.
Cohen, Herb. *Negotiate This!* New York, NY: Warner Books, Inc., 2003.
Cohen, Herb., *"You Can Negotiate Anything,"* Bantam Books, 1982.
Craver, C., *The Intelligent Negotiator*, Prima Venture, 2002.
Dawson, R., *El Arte de la Negociación,* Selectron, 2001.
Ertel, D., "Turning Negotiation into a Corporate Capability," *Harvard Business Review*, (May-June), 1999, 55-70.
Fisher, R., *Beyond Machiavelli*. Penguin Books, 1996.
Fisher, R. and Brown, S., *Getting Together. Building Relationships as We Negotiate*, Penguin Books, 1989.
Fisher, R., Ury, W. and Patton, B. *Getting to Yes*, Penguin Books, 1991.

Foster, D.A. *Bargaining Across Borders: How to Negotiate Business Successfully Anywhere in the World*, McGraw Hill, 1992, 264-293.

Gelfand, M., and Brett, J., *The Handbook of Negotiation and Culture*, Standford Business Books, 2004.

Graham, J.L. and Herberger, R.A.Jr., "Negotiators Abroad Don't Shoot From the Hip." *Harvard Business Review,* (July-August), 1983, 160-168.

Graham, J.L. and Adler, N.J., "Cross Cultural Interaction: The International Comparison Fallacy?", *Journal of International Business Studies,* **20**, 1989, 515-537.

Graham, J.L. and Cateora, P.R., *International Marketing*, 11th edition, NY: McGraw-Hill, 1999, Chapter 19.

Gray, J., *Men are from Mars and Women are from Venus*, Harper Collins, 1992.

Harvard Business Review: On Negotiation and Conflict Resolution, HBSP, 2000.

Hawkins,D., *Power vs. Force*, Hay House, 2002.

Hofstede, G., *Culture's Consequences: International Differences in Work- Related Values*, Sage Publications, 1980.

Hofstede, G., *Cultures and Organizations: Software of the Mind: Intercultural Cooperation and its Importance for Survival*, HarperCollins, 1994.

Hofstede, G., The Business of International Business is Culture, in: Jackson, T. (ed.) *Cross Cultural Management*, Butterworth Heinemann Ltd, 1995, 150-165.

Hofstede, G., "*Levels of Culture and National Cultures in Four Dimensions,*" in Hickson, D. (ed.) *Exploring Management Across the World*, Penguin Group, 1997, Chapter 1, pp. 3-13.

Karras, C., *The Negotiating Game*, Harper Business, 1992.

Lax, David A. and Sebenius, James K., *The Manager as Negotiator*, The Free Press, 1986.

Lewicki, Roy J., Saunders, David M. and Minton, John W., *Negotiation: Readings, Exercises, and Cases*, 2nd ed., McGraw Hill, 1994, Chapter 4, pp. 80-108.

Mackay, H., *Swim with the Sharks Without Being Eaten Alive*, Ballantine Books, 1988.

Morrison, T., Conaway, W and Douress, J., *Doing Business Around The World,* Dun & Bradstreet's Guide by Prentice Hall, Inc, 1997.
Nierenberg, G., *The Art of Negotiating,* Barnes and Noble books, 1995.
Nierenberg, G., *The Complete Negotiator*, Barnes and Noble books, 1986.
Nierenberg, G., *The Art of Creative Thinking*, Barnes and Noble books, 1996.
Pekar, A., and Colson, A., *Méthode de Négociation*, Dunod, 2004.
Pruitt, D.G. and Rubin J.Z., *Social Conflict: Escalation, Stalemate, and Settlement,* Random House, 1986.
Pruitt, D.G., "Strategy in Negotiation," in Jossey Bass Publishers, (ed.) *International Negotiation: Analysts, Approaches, Issues,* Jossey Bass Inc., 1991, Chapter 6, pp. 78-89.
Raiffa, H., *The Art and Science of Negotiation,* The Belknap Press of Harvard University Press, 2000.
Salacuse, J., *The Wise Advisor,* Praeger Publishers, 2000.
Salacuse, J., *Making Global Deals: What Every Executive Should Know About Negotiating Abroad,* Times Business, 1991.
Salacuse, J., *The Global Negotiator: Making, Managing and Mending Deals Around the World in the 21st Century*, Times Business, 2000.
Salacuse, J. W., "Ten Ways That Culture Affects Negotiating Style: Some Survey Results," *Negotiation Journal,* (July) 1998, 221-240.
Savage, G., Blair, J. and Sorenson, R., *Academy of Management Executive* **3** (1), 1989.
Selva, Chantal, *La PNL Aplicada a la Negociación*, Granica, 1998.
Shell, G., *Bargaining for Advantage*, Penguin Books, 2006
Slate, F., "Tips For Negotiations in Germany and France", *HR Focus*, **71** (7), 1994.
Stark, P., *Todo es Negociable,* McGraw-Hill, 1995.
Stone, D., Patton, B. and Heen. S., *Difficult Conversations*, Penguin Books, 2000.
Susskind, L. and Field, P., *Dealing with an Angry Public. The Mutual Gains Approach to Resolving Disputes*, Free Press, 1996.

Susskind, L., McKearnan, S., and Thomas-Larmer, J., *The Consensus Building Handbook*, Sage Publications, 1999.

Thompson, L., "Information Exchange in Negotiation", *Journal of Experimental Social Psychology*, **27**, 1991, 161-179.

Thompson, L., *The Mind and Heart of the Negotiator*, Pearson, 2005.

Ury, W., *Getting Past No,* Bantam Books, 1991.

Ury, W., *The Third Side,* Penguin Books, 2000.

Volkema, R. and Chang, S., "Negotiating in Latin America: What We Know (or Think We Know) and What We Would Like to Know," *Latin American Business Review*, **1** (2), 1998, 3-25.

Walton, Richard E. and McKersie, Robert, B. A., *Behavioural Theory of Labour Negotiations,* McGraw Hill, 1965.

Watkins, M., *Breakthrough Business Negotiations, a Toolbox for Managers*, Jossey-Bass, 2002.

Wheeler, M., *Teaching Negotiation: Ideas and Innovations*, Program on Negotiation at Harvard Law School, 2000.

Williams, R., *Latin Quips at your Fingertips*, Barnes and Noble, 2001.

Wriggins, H.W., *Up for Auction: Malta Bargains with Great Britain, 1971,* in W. Zartman (ed.), *The Fifty Percent Solution*, Anchor Press, 1976, 208-234.

Young, P., *Negotiation Analysis,* in Young, P. (ed.) *Negotiation Analysis*, The University of Michigan Press, 1994, Chapter 1, pp. 1-23.

Zartman, I.W., "The Structure of Negotiation," in Jossey Bass Publishers (ed.) *International Negotiation: Analysis, Approaches, Issues*, Jossey Bass Inc, 1991, Chapter 5, pp. 65-77.

Ziglar, Z., *ZIG ZIGLAR'S Secrets of Closing the Sale,* Berkley Books, 1985.

About the Collaborator
Randy Doyle Hazlett, Ph.D.

Dr. Hazlett is a seasoned technical writer and communicator. He is the President of *Potential Research Solutions* and *Christian Artist's Workshop*. He has extensive industrial experience in bringing cutting-edge R&D to standard business practice. Dr. Hazlett earned his doctorate degree in Chemical Engineering from the University of Texas at Austin. His contribution to this book brings together his business savvy, technical editorial skills, and knowledge of biblical history. Dr. Hazlett is a long-time personal friend and business partner of Dr. Habib Chamoun-Nicolás.

Dr. Hazlett is the holder of 12 U. S. Patents. He has authored 30+ Domestic & International Technical Symposia Presentations, 25+ Technical Journal Publications, 3 Trade Book Entries, and a series of ebooks. Dr. Hazlett's latest independent effort for publication through Christian Artist's Workshop, *The Pilgrimage and Dark Spaces – Collected Short Works of Fictional Drama*, is sure to become a masterwork.

About the Author
Dr. Habib Chamoun-Nicolás

Over two decades, Dr. Chamoun-Nicolás has been conducting negotiation and business development activities in diversified sectors (industrial, commercial, government, institutional) for the sales and marketing of services and products. He has worked for ELF Aquitaine, ICA Fluor Daniel, and Brown and Root. Dr. Chamoun has trained thousands business and government professionals on *A Business Development Approach on Sales and Negotiation* and has conducted extensive research on *How Mexicans Negotiate*.

Dr. Chamoun-Nicolás graduated from University of Texas at Austin and the Monterrey Institute of Technology and has participated in several special executive programs, such as the Program on Negotiation at Harvard University and the Brazilian Seminar at the International School of Business at the University of South Carolina. Dr. Chamoun has also been an invited guest speaker and instructor at several universities: Thunderbird School of International Business in the GLOBAL MBA program, MBOC at the University of Texas, PANAM, University of Texas Dallas Cohort MBA program, and the University of Houston on Negotiation and Business development related topics. Dr Chamoun has participated as a professor at the Virtual University of the Monterrey Institute of Technology in Mexico. The Autonomous University of Honduras, Business International School of San Pedro Sula and Catholic University of Guayaquil

Ecuador are among the Central and Latin America Universities were he has taught negotiation. He is the author of many articles on negotiation and the books: *Desarrollo de Negocios*, in its 3rd edition, *Trato Hecho-Guía para una Negociación sin Fallas* (2nd edition) and *DEAL: Guidelines for a Flawless Negotiation* (a special edition on Culture and Negotiation, 3rd edition, *in English*).

A partial list of his commercial and industrial clients includes: Exxon-Mobil, Marathon Oil Company, Halliburton, Dynasol (Repsol / Grupo Desc), Telmex, Telcel, Axtel (Bell Canada), Maxcom, Sears, Banorte, Banrural, Jugos del Valle, USA, Bimbo Snacks, USA, T-Systems International, AMECO (equipment branch of Fluor Daniel Corp), AIT Group Mexico, Baxter, Grace Davison, RSM BEPAM, Santa Marina y Esteta Abogados, Henkel, Celanese, Procter and Gamble, CAIC, Shell Oil, Franklin Covey, Grupo Educare, SGS Mexico, and others.

Dr. Chamoun is a member of the advisory board of the Frank Evans Center for Conflict Resolution at the South Texas School of Law. Also he is a board member of the American College of Acupuncture and Oriental Medicine, Genesys, ITS, and the CELH (Chamber of Latin entrepreneurs of Houston). Dr. Chamoun has been honored as the writer of the year 2006 at the 4th Hispanic Book Festival of Houston and he has been appointed by Major Bill White of Houston as a Council member of the Mayor's International Affairs & Development Council of the Americas. Dr. Habib Chamoun-Nicolás was awarded with the title of honorary professor at the Faculty of entrepreneurial specialties at the Catholic University of Santiago de Guayaquil.

Contacting the Author

Dr. Habib Chamoun-Nicolás
P.O. Box 6558
Kingwood, TX 77345
USA
(281) 360-8205
HChamoun@Keynegotiations.com *or*
glazez@Keynegotiations.com

Phoenicians Bartering with Ancient Britons, Lord Frederic Leighton, c. 1894-1895
fresco on canvas, The Royal Exchange, London
Reproduced by courtesy of the Joint Grand Gresham Committee

TraDEAbLes™

Tradeables™: A set of ideas or actions that help leverage a DEAL without being a part of the deal by placing perceived needs of the other party above the DEAL.

Famous Quotes:

You must give some time to your fellow men. Even if it's a little thing, do something for others – something for which you get no pay but the privilege of doing it. **Albert Schweitzer**

Anything we haven't seen before is marvelous. **Tacitus**

The whole cannot be well unless the parts are well. **Plato**

Good sense, not age, brings wisdom **Syrus, Maxims**

Anger is the one thing made better by delay. **Syrus, Maxims**

Be careful about starting something you may regret. **Syrus, Maxims**

It is better to trust in courage than in luck. **Syrus, Maxims**

For it is in giving that we receive. **St. Francis of Assisi**

When you have just climbed out of a deep well and are perched on top, you are in the greatest danger of falling again. **Plautus**

A man needs a good mirror to scrutinize his heart as well as his face. **Plautus**

Fortune favours the brave. **Terence**

The great thing is to know when to speak and when to keep quiet. **Seneca the youngest**

Shallowness is natural; conceit comes with education. **Cicero**

Never, never, never give up! **Winston Churchill.**

Wealth is above all an accumulation of possibilities. **Gabriel Zaid**

We give of ourselves when we give the gift of words: encouragement, inspiration, guidance. **Wilferd A. Peterson**